To:

_____

The LORD will guide
you always.

ISAIAH 58:11

From:

_____

God's Words of Life for Young Women of Faith
Copyright © 2003 Zondervan
ISBN 0-310-98885-3

All devotions taken from the: *Young Women of Faith Bible, New International Version.*® Copyright © 2001 by Zondervan. All rights reserved.

All Scripture quotations, unless otherwise noted, are taken from the *Holy Bible: New International Version,* (North American Edition). Copyright ©1973, 1978, 1984, by International Bible Society. Used by permission of Zondervan. All rights reserved.

The "NIV" and "New International Version" trademarks are registered in the United States Patent and Trademark Office by International Bible Society.

Requests for information should be addressed to:
Inspirio, The gift group of Zondervan
Grand Rapids, Michigan 49530
http://www.inspiriogifts.com

Compiler: Molly C. Detweiler
Project Manager/Editor: Janice Jacobson
Design Manager: Amy J. Wenger
Design: Amy Peterman/Peterman Design

Printed in China
03 04 05/HK/ 4 3 2

God's Words of Life for
Young Women
OF Faith

from the
New International Version

inspirio™

God's Word of Life on

God's Words of Life on

Belief

Who is it that overcomes the world? Only he who believes that Jesus is the Son of God.

❀ 1 JOHN 5:5

You ... were included in Christ when you heard the word of truth, the gospel of your salvation. Having believed, you were marked in him with a seal, the promised Holy Spirit, who is a deposit guaranteeing our inheritance until the redemption of those who are God's possession—to the praise of his glory.

❀ EPHESIANS 1:13-14

Jesus said, "If you believe, you will receive whatever you ask for in prayer."

❀ MATTHEW 21:22

From the beginning God chose you to be saved through the sanctifying work of the Spirit and through belief in the truth.

❀ 2 THESSALONIANS 2:13

God's Words of Life on

Belief

We believe that Jesus died and rose again and so we believe that God will bring with Jesus those who have fallen asleep in him. ... For the Lord himself will come down from heaven, with a loud command, with the voice of the archangel and with the trumpet call of God, and the dead in Christ will rise first. After that, we who are still alive and are left will be caught up together with them in the clouds to meet the Lord in the air. And so we will be with the Lord forever.

✿ 1 THESSALONIANS 4:14, 16-17

I pray ... that the eyes of your heart may be enlightened in order that you may know the hope to which God has called you, the riches of his glorious inheritance in the saints, and his incomparably great power for us who believe. That power is like the working of his mighty strength, which he exerted in Christ when he raised him from the dead and seated him at his right hand in the heavenly realms, far above all rule and authority, power and dominion, and every title that can be given, not only in the present age but also in the one to come.

✿ EPHESIANS 1:18-21

God's Words of Life on

Belief

Through Jesus you believe in God, who raised him from the dead and glorified him, and so your faith and hope are in God.

✿ **1 PETER 1:21**

If you confess with your mouth, "Jesus is Lord," and believe in your heart that God raised him from the dead, you will be saved. For it is with your heart that you believe and are justified, and it is with your mouth that you confess and are saved.

✿ **ROMANS 10:9-10**

Righteousness from God comes through faith in Jesus Christ to all who believe.

✿ **ROMANS 3:22**

I am not ashamed of the gospel, because it is the power of God for the salvation of everyone who believes.

✿ **ROMANS 1:16**

Devotional Thought on

Belief

CAN YOU BELIEVE
THE UNBELIEVABLE?

In the Bible, in the book of Mark, a father comes to Jesus for healing for his little boy. The boy's father has heard of Jesus and his disciples and the many people they have healed, so he brings his son to see Jesus. In Mark 9:22 the father says to Jesus, "If you can do anything, ... help us." When he says, "if you can," he shows that he doesn't really believe in Jesus. But he also shows that he wants to believe, because he asks Jesus to "help me overcome my unbelief!" (Mark 9:24)

Not believing in Jesus' power to do something can keep your faith from growing stronger. Like this boy's father, ask Jesus to help you defeat your unbelief.

Do you believe God can do anything? Think back over your life and look for times when God has helped you in ways you never thought he would. Ask family members if they have experienced amazing things God has done when doubt may have been hanging around. Then ask Jesus to help you believe. He will lovingly lend a hand just as he did with the father in Mark 9:23, "'If you can'?" said Jesus. "Everything is possible for him who believes."

God's Words of Life on

Comfort

Praise be to the God and Father of our Lord Jesus Christ, the Father of compassion and the God of all comfort, who comforts us in all our troubles, so that we can comfort those in any trouble with the comfort we ourselves have received from God.

✿ 2 CORINTHIANS 1:3-4

Blessed are those who mourn,
for they will be comforted.

✿ MATTHEW 5:4

"As a mother comforts her child,
so will I comfort you," says the Lord.

✿ ISAIAH 66:13

The ransomed of the LORD will return.
They will enter Zion with singing;
everlasting joy will crown their heads.
Gladness and joy will overtake them,
and sorrow and sighing will flee away.
"I, even I, am he who comforts you," says the Lord.

✿ ISAIAH 51:11-12

God's Words of Life on

Comfort

The Spirit of the Sovereign LORD is on me,
    because the LORD has anointed me
    to preach good news to the poor.
He has sent me to bind up the brokenhearted,
    to proclaim freedom for the captives
    and release from darkness for the prisoners,
to proclaim the year of the LORD'S favor
    and the day of vengeance of our God,
to comfort all who mourn,
    and provide for those who grieve in Zion—
to bestow on them a crown of beauty
    instead of ashes,
the oil of gladness
    instead of mourning,
and a garment of praise
    instead of a spirit of despair.

✿ ISAIAH 61:1-3

May your unfailing love be my comfort, O Lord,
    according to your promise to your servant.

✿ PSALM 119:76

God's Words of Life on

Comfort

Shout for joy, O heavens;
*   rejoice, O earth;*
*   burst into song, O mountains!*
For the LORD comforts his people
*   and will have compassion on his afflicted ones.*

✿ ISAIAH 49:13

The LORD your God is with you,
*   he is mighty to save.*
He will take great delight in you,
*   he will quiet you with his love,*
*   he will rejoice over you with singing.*

✿ ZEPHANIAH 3:17

This I call to mind
*   and therefore I have hope:*
Because of the LORD'S great love we are not consumed,
*   for his compassions never fail.*
They are new every morning;
*   great is your faithfulness.*

✿ LAMENTATIONS 3:21-23

God's Words of Life on

Comfort

Surely God is my salvation;
I will trust and not be afraid.
The LORD, the LORD, is my strength and my song;
he has become my salvation.

✿ ISAIAH 12:2

How priceless is your unfailing love, O Lord!
Both high and low among men
find refuge in the shadow of your wings.

✿ PSALM 36:7

You will increase my honor
and comfort me once again, O Lord.

✿ PSALM 71:21

Because you are my help,
I sing in the shadow of your wings, O Lord.
My soul clings to you;
your right hand upholds me.

✿ PSALM 63:7-8

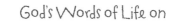

God's Words of Life on

Comfort

The LORD is my shepherd, I shall not be in want.
He makes me lie down in green pastures,
he leads me beside quiet waters,
he restores my soul.
He guides me in paths of righteousness
for his name's sake.
Even though I walk
through the valley of the shadow of death,
I will fear no evil,
for you are with me;
your rod and your staff,
they comfort me.
You prepare a table before me
in the presence of my enemies.
You anoint my head with oil;
my cup overflows.
Surely goodness and love will follow me
all the days of my life,
and I will dwell in the house of the LORD
forever.

✿ **PSALM 23**

Devotional Thought on

Comfort

GOD WILL ALWAYS
COMFORT YOU

You've been taught that God can be trusted, but maybe you aren't really sure. Jesus came to earth to show you God the Father. He wants you to know about God's love, gentleness, and kindness. Jesus is God the Son. When you know Jesus you also know the Father.

When you feel upset or afraid, do you have a favorite doll or bear you like to hold, or a place you like to go? Those things give you comfort. As you grow up, you will outgrow these comforting things. But we never outgrow God's comfort.

God comforts us in many ways. Sometimes it's something we read in the Bible. It may be something your mom or dad says, a friend, a teacher, or a pastor. Maybe it's something you read in a book or a thought that comes to you when you pray.

Are you having a rough time right now? Pray to God for help and for comfort. Trusting God allows you to enjoy all the surprises of life and to go through all the difficulties of life. You are always safe with God—no matter what happens.

God's Words of Life on

Courage

*Be strong and courageous. Do not be terrified; do
not be discouraged, for the LORD your God will be
with you wherever you go.*

❀ JOSHUA 1:9

*There is no fear in love. But perfect love drives
out fear.*

❀ 1 JOHN 4:18

*God has said,
"Never will I leave you;
    never will I forsake you."
So we say with confidence,
    "The Lord is my helper; I will not be afraid.
    What can man do to me?"*

❀ HEBREWS 13:5-6

*You did not receive a spirit that makes you a slave
again to fear, but you received the Spirit of sonship.
And by him we cry, "Abba, Father." The Spirit himself testifies with our spirit that we are God's children.*

❀ ROMANS 8:15-16

*Jesus said, "Do not be afraid, little flock, for your
Father has been pleased to give you the kingdom."*

❀ LUKE 12:32

16

God's Words of Life on

Courage

Jesus said, "Peace I leave with you; my peace I give you. I do not give to you as the world gives. Do not let your hearts be troubled and do not be afraid."

✿ **JOHN 14:27**

When I am afraid,
* I will trust in you.*
In God, whose word I praise,
* in God I trust; I will not be afraid.*

✿ **PSALM 56:3-4**

Are not five sparrows sold for two pennies? Yet not one of them is forgotten by God. Indeed, the very hairs of your head are all numbered. Don't be afraid; you are worth more than many sparrows.

✿ **LUKE 12:6-7**

You came near when I called you,
* and you said, "Do not fear."*
O Lord, you took up my case;
* you redeemed my life.*

✿ **LAMENTATIONS 3:57-58**

God's Words of Life on

Courage

Blessed is the man who trusts in the LORD,
*   whose confidence is in him.*
He will be like a tree planted by the water
*   that sends out its roots by the stream.*
It does not fear when heat comes;
*   its leaves are always green.*
It has no worries in a year of drought
*   and never fails to bear fruit.*

✿ JEREMIAH 17:7-8

This is what the LORD says ...
"Fear not, for I have redeemed you;
*   I have summoned you by name; you are mine.*
When you pass through the waters,
*   I will be with you;*
and when you pass through the rivers,
*   they will not sweep over you.*
When you walk through the fire,
*   you will not be burned;*
*   the flames will not set you ablaze."*

✿ ISAIAH 43:1-2

Devotional Thought on

Courage

FACING THE BIG GIANT

In 1 Samuel 17 we can read the story of David and a big giant named Goliath. Goliath is one big, strong dude, with big, strong armor besides! Goliath makes fun of the Lord! (1 Samuel 17:26) The King of God's people, Saul, and his army, are terrified!

Then along comes a little shepherd boy named David. Goliath doesn't scare David, because David doesn't rely on his own strength. He trusts in the power of the real God.

When you trust God rather than yourself, you can depend on his help. People might not understand your confidence in a God they can't see. They may even try to talk you out of believing in God's strength, like people did to David. But stay strong. Keep trusting in God's abilities, not your own. And, like David, give God the credit for the outcome (1 Samuel 17:47).

Fear is an emotion everyone experiences. When you are afraid, say the same thing David did: "When I am afraid, I will trust in God" (Psalm 56:3). Try to see your fear as a time to grow in trust. It's a chance to run to the Lord and have your faith increase.

God's Words of Life on

Emotions

Is anyone happy? Let him sing songs of praise.

❀ JAMES 5:13

In my anguish I cried to the LORD,
and he answered by setting me free.

❀ PSALM 118:5

A happy heart makes the face cheerful.

❀ PROVERBS 15:13

May the righteous be glad and rejoice before God;
may they be happy and joyful.

❀ PSALM 68:3

Jesus said, "Come to me, all you who are weary and
burdened, and I will give you rest. Take my yoke
upon you and learn from me, for I am gentle and
humble in heart, and you will find rest for your
souls. For my yoke is easy and my burden is light."

❀ MATTHEW 11:28-30

God's Words of Life on

Emotions

Why are you downcast, O my soul?
Why so disturbed within me?
Put your hope in God,
for I will yet praise him,
my Savior and my God.

✿ PSALM 42:5-6

Though you have made me see troubles, many and bitter,
you will restore my life again;
from the depths of the earth
you will again bring me up.
You will increase my honor
and comfort me once again.

✿ PSALM 71:20-20

Blessed are those who mourn,
for they will be comforted.

✿ MATTHEW 5:4

God sets the lonely in families.

✿ PSALM 68:6

21

God's Words of Life on

Emotions

Turn to me and be gracious to me, LORD,
for I am lonely and afflicted.
The troubles of my heart have multiplied;
free me from my anguish.
Look upon my affliction and my distress
and take away all my sins. ...
Guard my life and rescue me;
let me not be put to shame,
for I take refuge in you.
May integrity and uprightness protect me,
because my hope is in you.

✿ PSALM 25:16-18, 20-21

When I am afraid,
I will trust in you, O LORD.

✿ PSALM 56:3

Everyone should be quick to listen, slow to speak
and slow to become angry.

✿ JAMES 1:19

22

Devotional Thought on

Emotions

GOOD MEDICINE

Do you ever wake up feeling grumpy? Does your mom say, "Did you get up on the wrong side of the bed?" Have you ever taken out your bad mood on your friends, even when it wasn't their fault? Probably everyone has done this sometime in her life!

Do you know you can change your mood? Everyone has troubles and disappointments sometimes, but we don't have to crawl into bed and give up hope. Instead we can decide we will trust God with our troubles.

Changing your attitude is "good medicine" (Proverbs 17:22). If you are happy, you can be good medicine to the people around you, too. Giving in to unhappiness can keep you from enjoying the good things God gives you. Remember that God loves you and is on your side, no matter what—that should bring a smile to your face and happiness to your heart!

God's Words of Life on

Encouragement

May our Lord Jesus Christ himself and God our Father, who loved us and by his grace gave us eternal encouragement and good hope, encourage your hearts and strengthen you in every good deed and word.

✿ 2 THESSALONIANS 2:16-17

Paul said, "I have great confidence in you; I take great pride in you. I am greatly encouraged; in all our troubles my joy knows no bounds."

✿ 2 CORINTHIANS 7:4

You are a shield around me, O LORD; you bestow glory on me and lift up my head.

✿ PSALM 3:3

You hear, O LORD, the desire of the afflicted; you encourage them, and you listen to their cry.

✿ PSALM 10:17

God's Words of Life on

Encouragement

Everything that was written in the past was written to teach us, so that through endurance and the encouragement of the Scriptures we might have hope.

✿ **ROMANS 15:4**

The LORD upholds all those who fall
and lifts up all who are bowed down.

✿ **PSALM 145:14**

Blessed is he whose help is the God of Jacob,
whose hope is in the LORD his God,
the Maker of heaven and earth,
the sea, and everything in them—
the LORD, who remains faithful forever.
He upholds the cause of the oppressed
and gives food to the hungry.
The LORD sets prisoners free,
the LORD gives sight to the blind,
the LORD lifts up those who are bowed down,
the LORD loves the righteous.

✿ **PSALM 146:5-8**

God's Words of Life on

Encouragement

I lift up my eyes to the hills—
*   where does my help come from?*
My help comes from the LORD,
*   the Maker of heaven and earth.*

❀ **PSALM 121:1-2**

The LORD himself goes before you and will be with
you; he will never leave you nor forsake you. Do not
be afraid; do not be discouraged.

❀ **DEUTERONOMY 31:8**

*   I was overcome by trouble and sorrow.*
Then I called on the name of the LORD:
*   "O LORD, save me!"*
The LORD is gracious and righteous;
*   our God is full of compassion.*
The LORD protects the simplehearted;
*   when I was in great need, he saved me.*

❀ **PSALM 116:3-6**

Devotional Thought on

Encouragement

DON'T BE DISCOURAGED

You study as hard as you can, but you still get a C- on the math test. You pray every day for your sick grandma, but she doesn't seem to be getting any better. Your friend's parents are getting divorced and you don't know how to help her feel better.

Life is harder than you think it will be. Do you want to be a conqueror, someone who overcomes the hard parts of life? You can overcome the discouragement that life sometimes brings because Jesus Christ won't allow anything to come between you and his strong, saving love. "Who is it that overcomes the world? Only he who believes that Jesus is the Son of God" (1 John 5:5).

When trials, lies, teasing, sickness, or terrible times come, don't be too scared and feel too down. God will give you strength to overcome the tough times and to feel encouraged. God will never give you more than you can handle, and he'll provide enough support to get you through anything. That's a promise!

God's Words of Life on

Faith

Everyone born of God overcomes the world. This is the victory that has overcome the world, even our faith.

✿ 1 JOHN 5:4

The LORD your God is God; he is the faithful God, keeping his covenant of love to a thousand generations of those who love him and keep his commands.

✿ DEUTERONOMY 7:9

Now for a little while you may have had to suffer grief in all kinds of trials. These have come so that your faith—of greater worth than gold, which perishes even though refined by fire—may be proved genuine and may result in praise, glory and honor when Jesus Christ is revealed.

✿ 1 PETER 1:6-7

To the faithful you show yourself faithful, O LORD, to the blameless you show yourself blameless.

✿ 2 SAMUEL 22:26

God's Words of Life on

Faith

Love the LORD, all his saints!
The LORD preserves the faithful.

✿ PSALM 31:23

Though you have not seen Jesus, you love him; and
even though you do not see him now, you believe in
him and are filled with an inexpressible and glorious
joy, for you are receiving the goal of your faith, the
salvation of your souls.

✿ 1 PETER 1:8-9

Since we have been justified through faith, we have
peace with God through our Lord Jesus Christ,
through whom we have gained access by faith into
this grace in which we now stand.

✿ ROMANS 5:1-2

Faithfulness springs forth from the earth,
and righteousness looks down from heaven.
The LORD will indeed give what is good,
and our land will yield its harvest.

✿ PSALM 85:11-12

God's Words of Life on

Faith

Praise be to the God and Father of our Lord Jesus Christ! In his great mercy he has given us new birth into a living hope through the resurrection of Jesus Christ from the dead, and into an inheritance that can never perish, spoil or fade—kept in heaven for you, who through faith are shielded by God's power until the coming of the salvation that is ready to be revealed in the last time.

✿ **1 PETER 1:3-5**

I will sing of the LORD'S great love forever;
with my mouth I will make your faithfulness
known through all generations.
I will declare that your love stands firm forever,
that you established your faithfulness
in heaven itself.

✿ **PSALM 89:1-2**

The prayer offered in faith will make the sick person well; the Lord will raise him up.

✿ **JAMES 5:15**

God's Words of Life on

Faith

Let us fix our eyes on Jesus, the author and perfecter of our faith, who for the joy set before him endured the cross, scorning its shame, and sat down at the right hand of the throne of God. Consider him who endured such opposition from sinful men, so that you will not grow weary and lose heart.

✿ HEBREWS 12:2-3

Faith is being sure of what we hope for and certain of what we do not see.

✿ HEBREWS 11:1

By faith Moses, when he had grown up, refused to be known as the son of Pharaoh's daughter. He chose to be mistreated along with the people of God rather than to enjoy the pleasures of sin for a short time. He regarded disgrace for the sake of Christ as of greater value than the treasures of Egypt, because he was looking ahead to his reward.

✿ HEBREWS 11:24-26

Let us hold unswervingly to the hope we profess, for God who promised is faithful.

✿ HEBREWS 10:23

God's Words of Life on

Faith

I have fought the good fight, I have finished the race, I have kept the faith. Now there is in store for me the crown of righteousness, which the Lord, the righteous Judge, will award to me on that day—and not only to me, but also to all who have longed for his appearing.

✿ 2 TIMOTHY 4:7-8

The Lord is faithful, and he will strengthen and protect you from the evil one.

✿ 2 THESSALONIANS 3:3

In Christ and through faith in him we may approach God with freedom and confidence.

✿ EPHESIANS 3:12

Jesus said, "I tell you the truth, if you have faith as small as a mustard seed, you can say to this mountain, 'Move from here to there' and it will move. Nothing will be impossible for you."

✿ MATTHEW 17:20

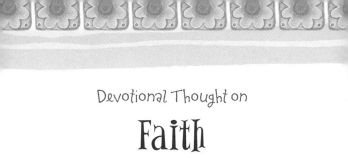

Devotional Thought on

Faith

WHAT IS FAITH?

Do you think you're a Christian because you can say you are? Do you think you are a Christian because your parents are? Knowing something just in your mind is not faith. So what is real faith? Romans 10:9 says, "If you confess with your mouth, 'Jesus is Lord,' and believe in your heart that God raised him from the dead, you will be saved."

Is your faith more than just knowing that there is a God? Really knowing Jesus is a belief that changes everything you do and makes you want to do what God wants you to do.

If you don't feel that God is your friend, ask him to be your friend. Jesus said, "Whoever comes to me I will never drive away" (John 6:37). Pray to God, asking him to help you depend on him more and more. Thank him for the gift of the Holy Spirit who helps us understand who Jesus is and to have faith in him. He will always help you when you ask him. You can have faith in that!

God's Words of Life on

Family

I have no greater joy than to hear that my children are walking in the truth.

✿ 3 JOHN 1:4

Both the one who makes men holy and those who are made holy are of the same family. So Jesus is not ashamed to call them brothers.

✿ HEBREWS 2:11

Children, obey your parents in the Lord, for this is right. "Honor your father and mother"—which is the first commandment with a promise—"that it may go well with you and that you may enjoy long life on the earth."

✿ EPHESIANS 6:1-3

As we have opportunity, let us do good to all people, especially to those who belong to the family of believers.

✿ GALATIANS 6:10

God's Words of Life on

Family

The Spirit himself testifies with our spirit that we are God's children. Now if we are children, then we are heirs—heirs of God and co-heirs with Christ, if indeed we share in his sufferings in order that we may also share in his glory.

✿ ROMANS 8:16-17

To all who received Christ, to those who believed in his name, he gave the right to become children of God-children born not of natural descent ... but born of God.

✿ JOHN 1:12-13

As a father has compassion on his children,
*   so the LORD has compassion*
*   on those who fear him.*

✿ PSALM 103:13

Children's children are a crown to the aged,
*   and parents are the pride of their children.*

✿ PROVERBS 17:6

God's Words of Life on

Family

From everlasting to everlasting
the LORD'S love is with those who fear him,
and his righteousness with their children's children—
with those who keep his covenant
and remember to obey his precepts.

✿ **PSALM 103:17-18**

For every house is built by someone, but God is the
builder of everything. Moses was faithful as a ser-
vant in all God's house, testifying to what would be
said in the future. But Christ is faithful as a son over
God's house. And we are his house, if we hold on to
our courage and the hope of which we boast.

✿ **HEBREWS 3:4-6**

Dear friends, let us love one another, for love comes
from God. Everyone who loves has been born of
God and knows God.

✿ **1 JOHN 4:7**

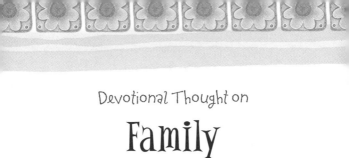

Devotional Thought on

Family

THE FAMILY OF GOD

Community means a group. The neighborhood you live in is a community. The church you go to is a community. But the first Christians were even closer. They depended on one another, and they shared everything! They met in the temple every day and studied and discussed the Word of God. They met in each other's homes to share meals, to pray together and to help each other. Everyone felt like part of the family of God. Blood relatives didn't mean being born to the same mother and father anymore. It meant being related through the blood of Christ.

Just think: God has not only provided you with the family you were born into, but he has also provided you with a huge family of brothers and sisters when you gave your heart to Jesus. Now God himself is your father. Family is a great blessing and a wonderful gift from God!

God's Words of Life on

Forgiveness

If we confess our sins, God is faithful and just and will forgive us our sins and purify us from all unrighteousness.

✿ 1 JOHN 1:9

When we were overwhelmed by sins,
    you forgave our transgressions, O LORD.

✿ PSALM 65:3

God has rescued us from the dominion of darkness and brought us into the kingdom of the Son he loves, in whom we have redemption, the forgiveness of sins.

✿ COLOSSIANS 1:13-14

If you, O LORD, kept a record of sins,
    O LORD, who could stand?
But with you there is forgiveness;
    therefore you are feared.
I wait for the LORD, my soul waits,
    and in his word I put my hope.

✿ PSALM 130:3-5

God's Words of Life on

Forgiveness

Let us draw near to God with a sincere heart in full assurance of faith, having our hearts sprinkled to cleanse us from a guilty conscience and having our bodies washed with pure water.

✿ **HEBREWS 10:22**

You are forgiving and good, O LORD,
abounding in love to all who call to you.

✿ **PSALM 86:5**

Everyone who believes in Jesus receives forgiveness of sins through his name.

✿ **ACTS 10:43**

Praise the LORD, O my soul,
and forget not all his benefits—
who forgives all your sins
and heals all your diseases.

✿ **PSALM 103:2-3**

God's Words of Life on

Forgiveness

I acknowledged my sin to you
and did not cover up my iniquity.
I said, "I will confess
my transgressions to the LORD"—
and you forgave
the guilt of my sin.
Therefore let everyone who is godly pray to you
while you may be found;
surely when the mighty waters rise,
they will not reach him.
You are my hiding place;
you will protect me from trouble
and surround me with songs of deliverance.

✿ PSALM 32:5-7

In Jesus we have redemption through his blood, the
forgiveness of sins, in accordance with the riches of
God's grace that he lavished on us with all wisdom
and understanding.

✿ EPHESIANS 1:7-8

God's Words of Life on

Forgiveness

As high as the heavens are above the earth,
    so great is God's love for those who fear him;
as far as the east is from the west,
    so far has he removed our transgressions from us.
As a father has compassion on his children,
    so the LORD has compassion
    on those who fear him.

✿ PSALM 103:11-13

"I will sprinkle clean water on you, and you will be clean; I will cleanse you from all your impurities. ... I will give you a new heart and put a new spirit in you; I will remove from you your heart of stone and give you a heart of flesh," says the LORD.

✿ EZEKIEL 36:25-26

Blessed is he
    whose transgressions are forgiven,
    whose sins are covered.
Blessed is the man
    whose sin the LORD does not count against him.

✿ PSALM 32:1-2

God's Words of Life on

Forgiveness

Cleanse me with hyssop, and I will be clean, O God;
*   wash me, and I will be whiter than snow.*

✿ PSALM 51:7

"Come now, let us reason together,"
*   says the LORD.*
"Though your sins are like scarlet,
*   they shall be as white as snow;*
though they are red as crimson,
*   they shall be like wool."*

✿ ISAIAH 1:18

Have mercy on me, O God,
*   according to your unfailing love;*
according to your great compassion
*   blot out my transgressions.*
Wash away all my iniquity
*   and cleanse me from my sin.*

✿ PSALM 51:1-2

Devotional Thought on

Forgiveness

GOD WILL ALWAYS
FORGIVE YOU

Did you know that you have a crown? It's a crown from God. This crown stands for God's gift to you of his love and compassion (Psalm 103:4). Compassion means gentleness and kindness— and forgiveness. God is your Father who wants to help you when you need him, and he wants to forgive you when you sin. His forgiveness is a wonderful gift!

Have you done something wrong and you really want to go back to God and ask for forgiveness, but you're afraid he doesn't want you or doesn't love you anymore? No matter what you have done, God loves you and he promises to forgive you when you ask him to. In 1 John 1:9 it says, "If we confess our sins, God is faithful and just and will forgive us our sins and purify us from all unrighteousness." So, why not go ahead and ask God to forgive you? He promises he will give you his very special gift of complete forgiveness.

God's Words of Life on

Friendship

A friend loves at all times.

✿ **PROVERBS 17:17**

There is a friend who sticks closer than a brother.

✿ **PROVERBS 18:24**

Perfume and incense bring joy to the heart,
*   and the pleasantness of one's friend springs*
from his earnest counsel.

✿ **PROVERBS 27:9**

Jesus said, "Greater love has no one than this, that
he lay down his life for his friends. You are my
friends if you do what I command. I no longer call
you servants, because a servant does not know his
master's business. Instead, I have called you friends,
for everything that I learned from my Father I have
made known to you."

✿ **JOHN 15:13-15**

Love one another deeply, from the heart.

✿ **1 PETER 1:22**

God's Words of Life on

Friendship

Two are better than one,
because they have a good return for their work:
If one falls down,
his friend can help him up.
But pity the man who falls
and has no one to help him up!
Also, if two lie down together, they will keep warm.
But how can one keep warm alone?
Though one may be overpowered,
two can defend themselves.
A cord of three strands is not quickly broken.

✿ ECCLESIASTES 4:9-12

As God's chosen people, holy and dearly loved,
clothe yourselves with compassion, kindness, humil-
ity, gentleness and patience. Bear with each other
and forgive whatever grievances you may have
against one another. Forgive as the Lord forgave
you. And over all these virtues put on love, which
binds them all together in perfect unity.

✿ COLOSSIANS 3:12-14

God's Words of Life on

Friendship

A kindhearted woman gains respect.

✿ **PROVERBS 11:16**

A generous man will prosper;
*   he who refreshes others will himself be*
refreshed.

✿ **PROVERBS 11:25**

An anxious heart weighs a man down,
*   but a kind word cheers him up.*

✿ **PROVERBS 12:25**

He who covers over an offense promotes love,
*   but whoever repeats the matter separates*
*   close friends.*

✿ **PROVERBS 17:9**

He who walks with the wise grows wise.

✿ **PROVERBS 13:20**

Devotional Thought on

Friendship

FRIENDS WITH GOD

Since you can't see God, it's not easy to be friends with him. After all, he doesn't sit with you and eat ice cream or talk with you on the phone. And sometimes it's hard to think of being friends with someone as powerful and holy as God. But remember, God isn't just mighty, he's also kind and loving. In the Bible he speaks of himself as a father and husband. Like a father, he loves his children and gives them the things they need. Like a husband, he wants to be your closest friend.

Do you have a best friend? You stay close friends because you talk to each other a lot, maybe even every day. One of the best ways to keep close to God is to talk to him by praying. Talk to him the same way you talk to your best friend. He is waiting to hear from you and to speak to your heart if you'll take time to listen. He wants to be your best friend!

God's Words of Life on

Future

"I know the plans I have for you," declares the LORD, "plans to prosper you and not to harm you, plans to give you hope and a future."

✿ **JEREMIAH 29:11**

Consider the blameless, observe the upright;
*   there is a future for the man of peace.*

✿ **PSALM 37:37**

Know also that wisdom is sweet to your soul;
*   if you find it, there is a future hope for you,*
*   and your hope will not be cut off.*

✿ **PROVERBS 24:14**

Many, O LORD my God,
*   are the wonders you have done.*
The things you planned for us
*   no one can recount to you;*
were I to speak and tell of them,
*   they would be too many to declare.*

✿ **PSALM 40:5**

God's Words of Life on

Future

Delight yourself in the LORD
and he will give you the desires of your heart.
Commit your way to the LORD;
trust in him and he will do this:
He will make your righteousness shine like the dawn,
the justice of your cause like the noonday sun.

✿ **PSALM 37:4-6**

No eye has seen,
no ear has heard,
no mind has conceived
what God has prepared for those who love him.

✿ **1 CORINTHIANS 2:9**

The LORD will fulfill his purpose for me;
your love, O LORD, endures forever.

✿ **PSALM 138:8**

Store up for yourselves treasures in heaven, where
moth and rust do not destroy, and where thieves do
not break in and steal. For where your treasure is,
there your heart will be also.

✿ **MATTHEW 6:20-21**

God's Words of Life on

Future

My frame was not hidden from you, LORD,
*   when I was made in the secret place.*
When I was woven together in the depths of the earth,
*   your eyes saw my unformed body.*
All the days ordained for me
*   were written in your book*
*   before one of them came to be.*

✿ **PSALM 139:15-16**

Forgetting what is behind and straining toward
what is ahead, I press on toward the goal to win the
prize for which God has called me heavenward in
Christ Jesus.

✿ **PHILIPPIANS 3:13-14**

Surely goodness and love will follow me
*   all the days of my life,*
and I will dwell in the house of the LORD
*   forever.*

✿ **PSALM 23:6**

Future

GOD'S GOOD PLANS

Do you ever think about the future? Do you wonder what you'll be like when you're older? Do you dream about your job or your future husband? It's fun to imagine what the future will be like. Jeremiah 29:11 is a favorite verse for many people—and it talks about your future. It says: "I know the plans I have for you," declares the LORD, "plans to prosper you and not to harm you, plans to give you hope and a future." It shows that God has plans for you. And not only plans—he has *good* plans for you!

When you don't know what the future holds, remember who holds the future. It is God. Ask him to help you know the things he wants you to do. Start by reading and studying the Bible—the Bible is the most important way God tells us what he wants us to do. Through his word he will guide you into the future he has planned—and *that* is the best future possible!

God's Words of Life on

God's Presence

I am convinced that neither death nor life, neither angels nor demons, neither the present nor the future, nor any powers, neither height nor depth, nor anything else in all creation, will be able to separate us from the love of God that is in Christ Jesus our Lord.

✿ **ROMANS 8:38-39**

Come near to God and he will come near to you.

✿ **JAMES 4:8**

"I am with you and will watch over you wherever you go. ... I will not leave you until I have done what I have promised you," says the Lord.

✿ **GENESIS 28:15**

No one has ever seen God; but if we love one another, God lives in us and his love is made complete in us.

✿ **1 JOHN 4:12**

God has said,
"Never will I leave you;
*   never will I forsake you."*

✿ **HEBREWS 13:5**

God's Words of Life on

God's Presence

Where can I go from your Spirit?
Where can I flee from your presence?
If I go up to the heavens, you are there, O LORD;
if I make my bed in the depths, you are there.
If I rise on the wings of the dawn,
if I settle on the far side of the sea,
even there your hand will guide me,
your right hand will hold me fast.

✿ PSALM 139:7-10

You have made known to me the path of life, O LORD;
you will fill me with joy in your presence,
with eternal pleasures at your right hand.

✿ PSALM 16:11

In my integrity you uphold me
and set me in your presence forever.
Praise be to the LORD, the God of Israel,
from everlasting to everlasting.

✿ PSALM 41:12-13

God's Words of Life on

God's Presence

Jesus said, "I will ask the Father, and he will give you another Counselor to be with you forever—the Spirit of truth. The world cannot accept him, because it neither sees him nor knows him. But you know him, for he lives with you and will be in you. I will not leave you as orphans; I will come to you."

✿ JOHN 14:16-18

"Fear not, for I have redeemed you;
*   I have summoned you by name; you are mine.*
When you pass through the waters,
*   I will be with you;*
and when you pass through the rivers,
*   they will not sweep over you.*
When you walk through the fire,
*   you will not be burned;*
*   the flames will not set you ablaze," says the* LORD.

✿ ISAIAH 43:1-2

Jesus said, "Surely I am with you always, to the very end of the age."

✿ MATTHEW 28:20

Devotional Thought on

God's Presence

THIRSTY FOR GOD

You know how it feels to be thirsty, don't you? Your mouth feels dry and yucky. All you can think about is finding a water fountain or running inside for a cold glass of water.

In Psalm 63, David uses needing water as a metaphor for his need for God. David knows how wonderful God is and he wants to keep enjoying God's friendship.

God is always with you, wherever you are. You may forget he's there, but he never forgets you. Speak to him like a friend—that's praying. In a journal or notebook, write about times when you feel God close to you. Write about his good gifts to you; write reasons to thank him and praise him for who he is and for what he has done. Build up your faith by writing about who Jesus is and what you mean to him. Because of Jesus, you can be friends with God!

So take time to "drink up" God's Word and you'll find that you don't feel thirsty deep down inside anymore!

God's Words of Life on

God's Will

Jesus said, "Whoever does God's will is my brother and sister and mother."

✿ MARK 3:35

Do not conform any longer to the pattern of this world, but be transformed by the renewing of your mind. Then you will be able to test and approve what God's will is—his good, pleasing and perfect will.

✿ ROMANS 12:2

The world and its desires pass away, but the man who does the will of God lives forever.

✿ 1 JOHN 2:17

Teach me to do your will,
*   for you are my God,*
may your good Spirit
*   lead me on level ground.*

✿ PSALM 143:10

God's Words of Life on

God's Will

Do not forget to do good and to share with others, for with such sacrifices God is pleased.

✿ HEBREWS 13:16

Jesus said, "I have come down from heaven not to do my will but to do the will of him who sent me. And this is the will of him who sent me, that I shall lose none of all that he has given me, but raise them up at the last day. For my Father's will is that everyone who looks to the Son and believes in him shall have eternal life, and I will raise him up at the last day."

✿ JOHN 6:38-40

May the God of peace ... equip you with everything good for doing his will, and may he work in us what is pleasing to him, through Jesus Christ, to whom be glory for ever and ever.

✿ HEBREWS 13:20-21

God's Words of Life on

God's Will

This is the confidence we have in approaching God: that if we ask anything according to his will, he hears us. And if we know that he hears us—whatever we ask—we know that we have what we asked of him.

✿ 1 JOHN 5:14-15

It is God who works in you to will and to act according to his good purpose.

✿ PHILIPPIANS 2:13

To the man who pleases him, God gives wisdom, knowledge and happiness.

✿ ECCLESIASTES 2:26

Be joyful always; pray continually; give thanks in all circumstances, for this is God's will for you in Christ Jesus.

✿ 1 THESSALONIANS 5:16

Devotional Thought on

God's Will

GETTING YOUR FEET WET

In Joshua 3:1-17 we read that Joshua and the Israelites stand at the edge of the Jordan River. Instead of its normal size of about a hundred feet wide, the river is flooded and the water is moving fast. It looks very difficult to cross. How can Joshua get all the people over to the other side? And if he can get them across, what direction should they go then?

God has a perfect plan. He will lead them himself. The priests are told to begin walking into the water until their feet are wet—then the waters of the river split apart the way the Red Sea had opened for Moses!

God promises good things to those who obey him and look for what his will is for them. Prayer is an important part of finding out what God wants you to do. Ask him for directions and listen to what he tells you through his Word. You may have to wait a while for God's answer, but be patient and don't give up on the one who knows you better than anyone else. God the Holy Spirit will help you think things through. But you might have to "get your feet wet" and start obeying what you know God wants you to do first, just like the priests did!

God's Words of Life on

Grace

Because of his great love for us, God, who is rich in mercy, made us alive with Christ even when we were dead in transgressions—it is by grace you have been saved.

✿ EPHESIANS 2:4-5

All have sinned and fall short of the glory of God, and are justified freely by his grace through the redemption that came by Christ Jesus.

✿ ROMANS 3:23-24

The LORD longs to be gracious to you;
he rises to show you compassion.
For the LORD is a God of justice.
Blessed are all who wait for him!

✿ ISAIAH 30:18

It is by grace you have been saved, through faith—and this not from yourselves, it is the gift of God—not by works, so that no one can boast.

✿ EPHESIANS 2:8-9

God's Words of Life on

Grace

Grace, mercy and peace from God the Father and from Jesus Christ, the Father's Son, will be with us in truth and love.

✿ 2 JOHN 1:3

You know the grace of our Lord Jesus Christ, that though he was rich, yet for your sakes he became poor, so that you through his poverty might become rich.

✿ 2 CORINTHIANS 8:9

The Word became flesh and made his dwelling among us. We have seen his glory, the glory of the One and Only, who came from the Father, full of grace and truth. ... From the fullness of his grace we have all received one blessing after another. For the law was given through Moses; grace and truth came through Jesus Christ.

✿ JOHN 1:14, 16-17

The LORD your God is gracious and compassionate. He will not turn his face from you if you return to him.

✿ 2 CHRONICLES 30:9

61

God's Words of Life on

Grace

God is able to make all grace abound to you, so that in all things at all times, having all that you need, you will abound in every good work.

✿ 2 CORINTHIANS 9:8

The LORD is compassionate and gracious,
slow to anger, abounding in love.
He will not always accuse,
nor will he harbor his anger forever;
he does not treat us as our sins deserve
or repay us according to our iniquities.
For as high as the heavens are above the earth,
so great is his love for those who fear him;
as far as the east is from the west,
so far has he removed our transgressions from us.
As a father has compassion on his children,
so the LORD has compassion
on those who fear him;
for he knows how we are formed,
he remembers that we are dust.

✿ PSALM 103:8-14

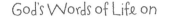

God's Words of Life on

Grace

When the kindness and love of God our Savior appeared, he saved us, not because of righteous things we had done, but because of his mercy. He saved us through the washing of rebirth and renewal by the Holy Spirit, whom he poured out on us generously through Jesus Christ our Savior, so that, having been justified by his grace, we might become heirs having the hope of eternal life.

✿ TITUS 3:4-7

God raised us up with Christ and seated us with him in the heavenly realms in Christ Jesus, in order that in the coming ages he might show the incomparable riches of his grace, expressed in his kindness to us in Christ Jesus.

✿ EPHESIANS 2:6-7

We do not have a high priest who is unable to sympathize with our weaknesses, but we have one who has been tempted in every way, just as we are—yet was without sin. Let us then approach the throne of grace with confidence, so that we may receive mercy and find grace to help us in our time of need.

✿ HEBREWS 4:15-16

God's Words of Life on

Grace

Grace and peace be yours in abundance through the knowledge of God and of Jesus our Lord. His divine power has given us everything we need for life and godliness through our knowledge of him who called us by his own glory and goodness.

✿ 2 PETER 1:2-3

To each one of us grace has been given as Christ apportioned it.

✿ EPHESIANS 4:7

God chose us in Christ before the creation of the world to be holy and blameless in his sight. In love he predestined us to be adopted as his sons through Jesus Christ, in accordance with his pleasure and will—to the praise of his glorious grace, which he has freely given us in the One he loves. In him we have redemption through his blood, the forgiveness of sins, in accordance with the riches of God's grace that he lavished on us with all wisdom and understanding.

✿ EPHESIANS 1:4-8

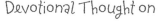

Devotional Thought on

Grace

A GREAT GIFT

Grace means God gives us something good we don't deserve. Let's say you make a deal with your mom or dad to clean the garage for $5, and when you finish the job, you get $10. That extra $5 is grace—it's a gift.

When someone shows you grace, how do you feel? You probably want to thank that person and you want to please him or her. In the same way, we thank God for showing us his grace in Jesus by praising him, and we try to please him because he's done so much good for us.

Make a list of ten good things God has given you. Share your list with your mom or dad or a good friend, and thank God for all the grace he has given you!

Here are a few ideas to get you started on your list:
- ✿ Parents
- ✿ The Bible
- ✿ Your health
- ✿ A good church
- ✿ Good friends
- ✿ Pets
- ✿ Brothers and sisters
- ✿ Fun toys

God's Words of Life on

Growth

Like newborn babies, crave pure spiritual milk, so that by it you may grow up in your salvation, now that you have tasted that the Lord is good.

✿ **1 Peter 2:2-3**

Speaking the truth in love, we will in all things grow up into him who is the Head, that is, Christ. From him the whole body, joined and held together by every supporting ligament, grows and builds itself up in love, as each part does its work.

✿ **Ephesians 4:15-16**

The righteous will flourish like a palm tree,
      they will grow like a cedar of Lebanon;
planted in the house of the LORD,
      they will flourish in the courts of our God.
They will still bear fruit in old age,
      they will stay fresh and green,
proclaiming, "The LORD is upright;
      he is my Rock, and there is no wickedness in him."

✿ **Psalm 92:12-15**

God's Words of Life on

Growth

Blessed are those who have learned to acclaim you,
*who walk in the light of your presence, O L*ORD.
They rejoice in your name all day long;
they exult in your righteousness.

✿ **P**SALM **89:15-16**

*Your hands made me and formed me, L*ORD;
give me understanding to learn your commands.

✿ **P**SALM **119:73**

Instruct a wise man and he will be wiser still;
teach a righteous man
and he will add to his learning.
*"The fear of the L*ORD *is the beginning of wisdom,*
and knowledge of the Holy One is understanding."

✿ **P**ROVERBS **9:9-10**

All Scripture is God-breathed and is useful for
teaching, rebuking, correcting and training in
righteousness, so that the man of God may be
thoroughly equipped for every good work.

✿ **2 T**IMOTHY **3:16-17**

God's Words of Life on

Growth

Anyone who lives on milk, being still an infant, is not acquainted with the teaching about righteousness. But solid food is for the mature, who by constant use have trained themselves to distinguish good from evil. Therefore let us leave the elementary teachings about Christ and go on to maturity.

✿ HEBREWS 5:13-6:1

If any of you lacks wisdom, he should ask God, who gives generously to all without finding fault, and it will be given to him.

✿ JAMES 1:5

It was God who gave some to be apostles, some to be prophets, some to be evangelists, and some to be pastors and teachers, to prepare God's people for works of service, so that the body of Christ may be built up until we all reach unity in the faith and in the knowledge of the Son of God and become mature, attaining to the whole measure of the fullness of Christ.

✿ EPHESIANS 4:11-13

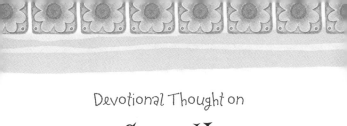

Devotional Thought on

Growth

MAKE GOD HAPPY

You can make God's day. Second Peter 1:5-8 says, "Make every effort to add to your faith goodness; and to goodness, knowledge; and to knowledge, self-control; and to self-control, perseverance; and to perseverance, godliness; and to godliness, brotherly kindness; and to brotherly kindness, love. For if you possess these qualities in increasing measure, they will keep you from being ineffective and unproductive in your knowledge of our Lord Jesus Christ." If you believe in Jesus Christ, God has given you everything you need for living a life that God would want you to.

Here is a list of ways you can keep growing in your relationship with Jesus:
Faith—Read your Bible at least once a week.
Perseverance—Keep studying in your least favorite subject in school.
Love—Tell your Mom and your Dad that "you" love them at least once a week.

Write down your own goals on how you will grow in these areas:
Goodness—
Knowledge—
Self-control—
Godliness—
Kindness—

God's Words of Life on

Guidance

The LORD will guide you always;
he will satisfy your needs in a sun-scorched land
and will strengthen your frame.
You will be like a well-watered garden,
like a spring whose waters never fail.

✿ ISAIAH 58:11

God is our God for ever and ever;
he will be our guide even to the end.

✿ PSALM 48:14

When he, the Spirit of truth, comes, he will guide
you into all truth. He will not speak on his own; he
will speak only what he hears, and he will tell you
what is yet to come.

✿ JOHN 16:13

The integrity of the upright guides them.

✿ PROVERBS 11:3

You guide me with your counsel, LORD,
and afterward you will take me into glory.

✿ PSALM 73:24

God's Words of Life on

Guidance

Keep your father's commands
and do not forsake your mother's teaching.
Bind them upon your heart forever;
fasten them around your neck.
When you walk, they will guide you;
when you sleep, they will watch over you;
when you awake, they will speak to you.
For these commands are a lamp,
this teaching is a light,
and the corrections of discipline
are the way to life.

✿ PROVERBS 6:20-23

If I rise on the wings of the dawn,
if I settle on the far side of the sea,
even there your hand will guide me, LORD,
your right hand will hold me fast.
If I say, "Surely the darkness will hide me
and the light become night around me,"
even the darkness will not be dark to you;
the night will shine like the day,
for darkness is as light to you.

✿ PSALM 139:9-12

God's Words of Life on

Guidance

Send forth your light and your truth, LORD,
    let them guide me;
let them bring me to your holy mountain,
    to the place where you dwell.

✿ PSALM 43:3

Good and upright is the LORD;
    therefore he instructs sinners in his ways.
He guides the humble in what is right
    and teaches them his way.
All the ways of the LORD are loving and faithful
    for those who keep the demands of his covenant.

✿ PSALM 25:8-10

In your unfailing love you will lead
    the people you have redeemed, O LORD.
In your strength you will guide them
    to your holy dwelling.

✿ EXODUS 15:13

God's Words of Life on

Guidance

*Direct me in the path of your commands, L*ORD*,
    for there I find delight.
Turn my heart toward your statutes
    and not toward selfish gain.
Turn my eyes away from worthless things;
    preserve my life according to your word.*

✿ **P**SALM **119:35-37**

*Show me your ways, O L*ORD*,
    teach me your paths;
guide me in your truth and teach me,
    for you are God my Savior,
    and my hope is in you all day long.*

✿ **P**SALM **25:4-5**

*This is what the L*ORD *says—
    your Redeemer, the Holy One of Israel:
"I am the L*ORD *your God,
    who teaches you what is best for you,
    who directs you in the way you should go."*

✿ **I**SAIAH **48:17**

God's Words of Life on

Guidance

This is what the LORD says:
"Stand at the crossroads and look;
ask for the ancient paths,
ask where the good way is, and walk in it,
and you will find rest for your souls."

✿ JEREMIAH 6:16

"I will give you shepherds after my own heart, who
will lead you with knowledge and understanding,"
says the LORD.

✿ JEREMIAH 3:15

Let the morning bring me word of your unfailing love,
for I have put my trust in you, O LORD.
Show me the way I should go,
for to you I lift up my soul.

✿ PSALM 143:8

Since you are my rock and my fortress, O God,
for the sake of your name lead and guide me.

✿ PSALM 31:3

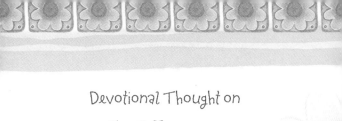

Devotional Thought on

Guidance

MAKING DECISIONS

You make many decisions every day—what to wear, who to eat lunch with, what extra activities to do at school. You will make major decisions a few times in your life—what college to go to, whom you will marry, where you will work.

Abraham's servant had the job of making a major decision for Isaac. He set out on a wife-finding mission. But he didn't leave the choice of a wife for Isaac to chance. Instead, he gave the decision to God. Without hesitating, he went to God for help to do this important thing. God heard his prayer and answered him, just as he has promised to hear and answer ours when we pray to him in faith (Psalm 17:6).

Before you make big or small decisions, pray for God's help. Ask him to help you know what to do. He will guide you to make the right choice.

God's Words of Life on

Hard Times

For Christ's sake, I delight in weaknesses, in insults, in hardships, in persecutions, in difficulties. For when I am weak, then I am strong.

✿ **2 CORINTHIANS 12:10**

The LORD is a refuge for the oppressed,
a stronghold in times of trouble.

✿ **PSALM 9:9**

If you are insulted because of the name of Christ, you are blessed, for the Spirit of glory and of God rests on you. ... If you suffer as a Christian, do not be ashamed, but praise God that you bear that name.

✿ **1 PETER 4:14, 16**

[Trials] have come so that your faith—of greater worth than gold, which perishes even though refined by fire—may be proved genuine and may result in praise, glory and honor when Jesus Christ is revealed.

✿ **1 PETER 1:7**

God's Words of Life on

Hard Times

Consider it pure joy ... whenever you face trials of many kinds, because you know that the testing of your faith develops perseverance. Perseverance must finish its work so that you may be mature and complete, not lacking anything.

✿ JAMES 1:2-4

This I call to mind
*   and therefore I have hope:*
Because of the LORD's great love we are not consumed,
*   for his compassions never fail.*
They are new every morning;
*   great is your faithfulness.*
I say to myself, "The LORD is my portion;
*   therefore I will wait for him."*
The LORD is good to those whose hope is in him,
*   to the one who seeks him;*
it is good to wait quietly
*   for the salvation of the LORD.*

✿ LAMENTATIONS 3:21-26

God's Words of Life on

Hard Times

Endure hardship as discipline. ... No discipline seems pleasant at the time, but painful. Later on, however, it produces a harvest of righteousness and peace for those who have been trained by it.

✿ HEBREWS 12:7, 11

Who shall separate us from the love of Christ? Shall trouble or hardship or persecution or famine or nakedness or danger or sword? ... No, in all these things we are more than conquerors through him who loved us.

✿ ROMANS 8:35, 37

We say with confidence,
"The Lord is my helper;
    I will not be afraid.
What can man do to me?"

✿ HEBREWS 13:6

Because Jesus himself suffered when he was tempted, he is able to help those who are being tempted.

✿ HEBREWS 2:18

God's Words of Life on

Hard Times

Our struggle is not against flesh and blood, but against the rulers, against the authorities, against the powers of this dark world and against the spiritual forces of evil in the heavenly realms. Therefore put on the full armor of God, so that when the day of evil comes, you may be able to stand your ground, and after you have done everything, to stand. Stand firm then, with the belt of truth buckled around your waist, with the breastplate of righteousness in place, and with your feet fitted with the readiness that comes from the gospel of peace. In addition to all this, take up the shield of faith, with which you can extinguish all the flaming arrows of the evil one. Take the helmet of salvation and the sword of the Spirit, which is the word of God.

❀ EPHESIANS 6:12-17

God has not despised or disdained
       the suffering of the afflicted one;
he has not hidden his face from him
       but has listened to his cry for help.

❀ PSALM 22:24

God's Words of Life on

Hard Times

With your help I can advance against a troop;
    with my God I can scale a wall.

✿ PSALM 18:29

In my alarm I said,
    "I am cut off from your sight!"
Yet you heard my cry for mercy
    when I called to you for help, O LORD.

✿ PSALM 31:22

I waited patiently for the LORD;
    he turned to me and heard my cry.
He lifted me out of the slimy pit,
    out of the mud and mire;
he set my feet on a rock
    and gave me a firm place to stand.
He put a new song in my mouth,
    a hymn of praise to our God.

✿ PSALM 40:1-3

Devotional Thought on

Hard Times

WHAT DO I DO
WHEN LIFE IS HARD?

Do you ever feel like you are hopeless and alone? Are there hard things happening in your family or school? Do you feel afraid and unsure of what to do? Do you ever feel like God is too far away to help you?

It's hard to understand, but the truth is that many children suffer. They don't deserve to. You don't deserve to. If you are in trouble, pray to God and tell him you need help. Be honest with him. Ask him to help you find someone to help you. Is there a relative or a counselor at school or a pastor you can talk to?

Sometimes things happen to us that we can't find a way out of right away. But try to remember that you aren't alone. God is with you and sees and feels the things you suffer. Don't give up. Keep looking for ways to get the help you need. God promises to always be with you!

God's Words of Life on

Healing

Praise the LORD, O my soul,
and forget not all his benefits—
who forgives all your sins
and heals all your diseases,
who redeems your life from the pit
and crowns you with love and compassion,
who satisfies your desires with good things
so that your youth is renewed like the eagle's.

✿ PSALM 103:2-5

God heals the brokenhearted
and binds up their wounds.

✿ PSALM 147:3

The Messiah was pierced for our transgressions,
he was crushed for our iniquities;
the punishment that brought us peace was upon him,
and by his wounds we are healed.

✿ ISAIAH 53:5

God's Words of Life on

Healing

Heal me, O LORD, and I will be healed;
save me and I will be saved,
for you are the one I praise.

✿ JEREMIAH 17:14

Jesus himself bore our sins in his body on the tree, so
that we might die to sins and live for righteousness;
by his wounds you have been healed.

✿ 1 PETER 2:24

Is any one of you sick? He should call the elders of
the church to pray over him and anoint him with oil
in the name of the Lord. And the prayer offered in
faith will make the sick person well; the Lord will
raise him up. If he has sinned, he will be forgiven.
Therefore confess your sins to each other and pray
for each other so that you may be healed. The prayer
of a righteous man is powerful and effective.

✿ JAMES 5:14-16

God's Words of Life on

Healing

"For you who revere my name, the sun of righteousness will rise with healing in its wings," says the LORD.

✿ MALACHI 4:2

Blessed is he who has regard for the weak;
the LORD delivers him in times of trouble.
The LORD will protect him and preserve his life. ...
The LORD will sustain him on his sickbed
and restore him from his bed of illness.

✿ PSALM 41:1-3

Restore us, O God;
make your face shine upon us,
that we may be saved.

✿ PSALM 80:3

The God of all grace, who called you to his eternal glory in Christ, after you have suffered a little while, will himself restore you and make you strong, firm and steadfast.

✿ 1 PETER 5:10

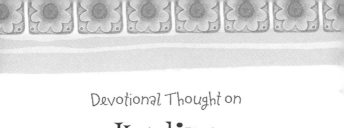

Devotional Thought on

Healing

GOD WILL DO
WHAT'S BEST FOR YOU

In John 9:1-7 Jesus does the unexpected to a blind man. He spits on the ground, makes a mud pie and puts it on the man's eyes. Then he tells the man to go to a certain pool of water and wash the mud from his eyes. Suppose the man had said, "Ick! I'm not going to walk through town with this mud pie on my face!" Do you think he would have been healed anyway?

We can't control most of the things that happen to us—just like the blind man couldn't control the fact that he went blind. Sometimes we get sick or hurt and there is nothing we can do to prevent it. But we do have God's word that "in all things God works for the good of those who love him" (Romans 8:28). When you are up against sickness or hurt that you don't understand, look for the way God is working for your good and your healing. Maybe you won't be able to see it—that's when you need to trust him. He promises to take care of you and heal you at just the right time.

God's Words of Life on

Heaven

I saw the Holy City, the new Jerusalem, coming down out of heaven from God, prepared as a bride beautifully dressed for her husband. And I heard a loud voice from the throne saying, "Now the dwelling of God is with men, and he will live with them. They will be his people, and God himself will be with them and be their God. He will wipe every tear from their eyes. There will be no more death or mourning or crying or pain, for the old order of things has passed away."

He who was seated on the throne said, "I am making everything new!" Then he said, "Write this down, for these words are trustworthy and true."

He said to me: "It is done. I am the Alpha and the Omega, the Beginning and the End. To him who is thirsty I will give to drink without cost from the spring of the water of life."

✿ REVELATION 21:2-6

In keeping with his promise we are looking forward to a new heaven and a new earth, the home of righteousness.

✿ 2 PETER 3:13

God's Words of Life on

Heaven

We believe that Jesus died and rose again and so we believe that God will bring with Jesus those who have fallen asleep in him. According to the Lord's own word, we tell you that we who are still alive, who are left till the coming of the Lord, will certainly not precede those who have fallen asleep. For the Lord himself will come down from heaven, with a loud command, with the voice of the archangel and with the trumpet call of God, and the dead in Christ will rise first. After that, we who are still alive and are left will be caught up together with them in the clouds to meet the Lord in the air. And so we will be with the Lord forever.

✿ 1 THESSALONIANS 4:14-17

[The angel] carried me away in the Spirit to a mountain great and high, and showed me the Holy City, Jerusalem, coming down out of heaven from God. It shone with the glory of God, and its brilliance was like that of a very precious jewel, like a jasper, clear as crystal.

✿ REVELATION 21:10-11

God's Words of Life on

Heaven

The Lord will rescue me from every evil attack and will bring me safely to his heavenly kingdom.

✿ 2 TIMOTHY 4:18

Our citizenship is in heaven. And we eagerly await a Savior from there, the Lord Jesus Christ.

✿ PHILIPPIANS 3:20

God raised us up with Christ and seated us with him in the heavenly realms in Christ Jesus, in order that in the coming ages he might show the incomparable riches of his grace, expressed in his kindness to us in Christ Jesus.

✿ EPHESIANS 2:6-7

Our light and momentary troubles are achieving for us an eternal glory that far outweighs them all. So we fix our eyes not on what is seen, but on what is unseen. For what is seen is temporary, but what is unseen is eternal.

✿ 2 CORINTHIANS 4:17-18

God's Words of Life on

Heaven

Jesus said, "Rejoice that your names are written in heaven."

❀ LUKE 10:20

Your word, O LORD, is eternal;
*   it stands firm in the heavens.*
Your faithfulness continues through all generations;
*   you established the earth, and it endures.*

❀ PSALM 119:89-90

Jesus said, "Blessed are you when men hate you,
when they exclude you and insult you and reject
your name as evil, because of the Son of Man.
Rejoice in that day and leap for joy, because great is
your reward in heaven."

❀ LUKE 6:22-23

Jesus said, "Let the little children come to me, and
do not hinder them, for the kingdom of heaven
belongs to such as these."

❀ MATTHEW 19:14

God's Words of Life on

Heaven

Jesus said, 'When the Son of Man comes in his glory, and all the angels with him, he will sit on his throne in heavenly glory. ...

Then the King will say to those on his right, 'Come, you who are blessed by my Father; take your inheritance, the kingdom prepared for you since the creation of the world. For I was hungry and you gave me something to eat, I was thirsty and you gave me something to drink, I was a stranger and you invited me in, I needed clothes and you clothed me, I was sick and you looked after me, I was in prison and you came to visit me.'"

"Then the righteous will answer him, 'Lord, when did we see you hungry and feed you, or thirsty and give you something to drink? When did we see you a stranger and invite you in, or needing clothes and clothe you? When did we see you sick or in prison and go to visit you?'

"The King will reply, 'I tell you the truth, whatever you did for one of the least of these brothers of mine, you did for me.'"

✿ **MATTHEW 25:31, 34-40**

Devotional Thought on

Heaven

JESUS' KINGDOM

A kingdom is where a king rules. The kingdom of heaven is ruled by Jesus Christ. Jesus says that his kingdom "is not of this world," but "is from another place" (John 18:36). But he also speaks of the kingdom of heaven here on earth (Matthew 12:28). The kingdom of heaven is wherever Jesus is king, even though we can't see him.

Do you feel sad about all the bad things that happen in our world? Are you tired of trying not to sin? There is something to look forward to, if you believe in the Lord Jesus. After you die, you will live in a perfect kingdom—forever. But even now you are part of that kingdom.

Remember to always make Jesus the king of your life and you will have a little taste of what heaven will be like, right here on earth!

God's Words of Life on

Hope

Even youths grow tired and weary,
*   and young men stumble and fall;*
but those who hope in the LORD
*   will renew their strength.*
They will soar on wings like eagles;
*   they will run and not grow weary,*
*   they will walk and not be faint.*

✿ ISAIAH 40:30-31

Jesus said, "Everything is possible for him who
believes."

✿ MARK 9:23

Dear friends, now we are children of God, and what
we will be has not yet been made known. But we
know that when Christ appears, we shall be like
him, for we shall see him as he is. Everyone who has
this hope in him purifies himself, just as he is pure.

✿ 1 JOHN 3:2-3

God has delivered us from such a deadly peril, and
he will deliver us. On him we have set our hope that
he will continue to deliver us.

✿ 2 CORINTHIANS 1:10

God's Words of Life on

Hope

The grace of God that brings salvation has appeared to all men. It teaches us to say "No" to ungodliness and worldly passions, and to live self-controlled, upright and godly lives in this present age, while we wait for the blessed hope—the glorious appearing of our great God and Savior, Jesus Christ, who gave himself for us to redeem us from all wickedness and to purify for himself a people that are his very own, eager to do what is good.

✿ TITUS 2:11-14

Through Christ you believe in God, who raised him from the dead and glorified him, and so your faith and hope are in God.

✿ 1 PETER 1:21

We wait in hope for the LORD;
        he is our help and our shield.
In him our hearts rejoice,
        for we trust in his holy name.
May your unfailing love rest upon us, O LORD,
        even as we put our hope in you.

✿ PSALM 33:20-22

God's Words of Life on

Hope

We know that in all things God works for the good of those who love him, who have been called according to his purpose. ... What, then, shall we say in response to this? If God is for us, who can be against us?

❀ ROMANS 8:28, 31

May our Lord Jesus Christ himself and God our Father, who loved us and by his grace gave us eternal encouragement and good hope, encourage your hearts and strengthen you in every good deed and word.

❀ 2 THESSALONIANS 2:16-17

Praise be to the God and Father of our Lord Jesus Christ! In his great mercy he has given us new birth into a living hope through the resurrection of Jesus Christ from the dead, and into an inheritance that can never perish, spoil or fade—kept in heaven for you, who through faith are shielded by God's power until the coming of the salvation that is ready to be revealed in the last time.

❀ 1 PETER 1:3-5

God's Words of Life on

Hope

*When the kindness and love of God our Savior
appeared, he saved us, not because of righteous
things we had done, but because of his mercy. He
saved us through the washing of rebirth and renewal
by the Holy Spirit, whom he poured out on us generously through Jesus Christ our Savior, so that, having been justified by his grace, we might become
heirs having the hope of eternal life.*

✿ TITUS 3:4-7

*No one whose hope is in you, LORD,
    will ever be put to shame*

✿ PSALM 25:3

*Find rest, O my soul, in God alone;
    my hope comes from him.
He alone is my rock and my salvation;
    he is my fortress, I will not be shaken.*

✿ PSALM 62:5-6

*I will always have hope;
    I will praise you more and more, LORD.*

✿ PSALM 71:14

God's Words of Life on

Hope

The LORD delights in those who fear him,
*   who put their hope in his unfailing love.*

✿ **PSALM 147:11**

Hope that is seen is no hope at all. Who hopes for
what he already has? But if we hope for what we do
not yet have, we wait for it patiently.

✿ **ROMANS 8:24-25**

Because God wanted to make the unchanging
nature of his purpose very clear to the heirs of what
was promised, he confirmed it with an oath. God did
this so that, by two unchangeable things in which it
is impossible for God to lie, we who have fled to take
hold of the hope offered to us may be greatly encour-
aged. We have this hope as an anchor for the soul,
firm and secure.

✿ **HEBREWS 6:17-19**

May the God of hope fill you with all joy and peace
as you trust in him, so that you may overflow with
hope by the power of the Holy Spirit.

✿ **ROMANS 15:13**

Devotional Thought on

Hope

A LIVING HOPE

A young woman is very sick, and there are no more ways to try to treat her. "I've given up hoping to get well," she says, "but my hope in the Lord will never die." Her hope to get well is a wish, but her hope in the Lord is much more than a wish. Christians have a living, eternal hope when they die.

Where does this hope come from? It comes when a person is born into God's family by believing in Jesus. We have this hope because Jesus came back from death to life. That's why it's a living hope—because Jesus lives, Christians will live, too.

If you do not have much hope right now, believe that God will make troubles into a "door of hope" (Hosea 2:15). God will take all your troubles and turn them into a door of hope within himself.

Take a minute to pray and imagine yourself handing your worries over to Jesus. See yourself walking through a doorway to Jesus. Let God's Holy Spirit fill you with a "living hope."

God's Words of Life on

Identity

We are God's workmanship, created in Christ Jesus to do good works, which God prepared in advance for us to do.

❁ **EPHESIANS 2:10**

Know that the LORD is God.
It is he who made us, and we are his;
we are his people, the sheep of his pasture.

❁ **PSALM 100:3**

When Christ, who is your life, appears, then you also will appear with him in glory.

❁ **COLOSSIANS 3:4**

What is man that you are mindful of him, O LORD,
the son of man that you care for him?
You made him a little lower than the heavenly beings
and crowned him with glory and honor.
You made him ruler over the works of your hands;
you put everything under his feet.

❁ **PSALM 8:4-6**

God's Words of Life on

Identity

*Jesus said, "Are not five sparrows sold for two
pennies? Yet not one of them is forgotten by God.
Indeed, the very hairs of your head are all
numbered. Don't be afraid; you are worth more
than many sparrows."*

✿ LUKE 12:6-7

*How great is the love the Father has lavished on us,
that we should be called children of God! And that
is what we are!*

✿ 1 JOHN 3:1

*"I will be a Father to you, and you will be my sons
and daughters," says the Lord Almighty.*

✿ 2 CORINTHIANS 6:18

*We are God's fellow workers; you are God's field,
God's building.*

✿ 1 CORINTHIANS 3:9

God's Words of Life on

Identity

The Spirit himself testifies with our spirit that we are God's children. Now if we are children, then we are heirs—heirs of God and co-heirs with Christ, if indeed we share in his sufferings in order that we may also share in his glory.

✿ ROMANS 8:16-17

Just as each of us has one body with many members, and these members do not all have the same function, so in Christ we who are many form one body, and each member belongs to all the others.

✿ ROMANS 12:4-5

"See, I have engraved you on the palms of my hands," says the LORD.

✿ ISAIAH 49:16

God created man in his own image, in the image of God he created him; male and female he created them.

✿ GENESIS 1:27

God's Words of Life on

Identity

You created my inmost being;
  you knit me together in my mother's womb.
I praise you because I am fearfully
    and wonderfully made;
  your works are wonderful,
  I know that full well.

✿ PSALM 139:13-14

We are the temple of the living God. As God has said: "I will live with them and walk among them, and I will be their God, and they will be my people."

✿ 2 CORINTHIANS 6:16

In God we live and move and have our being.

✿ ACTS 17:28

You have been born again, not of perishable seed, but of imperishable, through the living and enduring word of God.

✿ 1 PETER 1:23

God's Words of Life on

Identity

"Fear not, for I have redeemed you;
I have summoned you by name; you are mine,"
says the Lord.

✿ **ISAIAH 43:1**

From the beginning God chose you to be saved
through the sanctifying work of the Spirit and
through belief in the truth.

✿ **2 THESSALONIANS 2:13**

As you come to him, the living Stone—rejected by
men but chosen by God and precious to him—you
also, like living stones, are being built into a spiritual
house to be a holy priesthood, offering spiritual sacri-
fices acceptable to God through Jesus Christ.

✿ **1 PETER 2:4-5**

The LORD your God is with you,
*   he is mighty to save.*
He will take great delight in you,
*   he will quiet you with his love*
*   he will rejoice over you with singing.*

✿ **ZEPHANIAH 3:17**

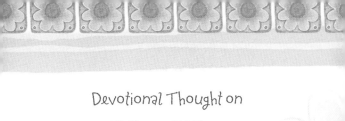

Devotional Thought on

Identity

THE GOD WHO SINGS

Imagine you are listening to God sing about you.
Do you think it sounds like the mighty roar of
thunder, or like a soft and gentle whisper? God
sings about you because he *loves* you! Think about
that. God sings with joy over you!

Yes, even though you do bad things, God loves
you. He knows everything about you, so he's not
surprised when you sin. That's the very reason Jesus
came! If you believe in Jesus, you are God's daughter—you belong to him and he will never stop loving you!

God rejoices over you and wants to give you
freedom, forgiveness, a new heart and spirit, his
very own Spirit to help you obey, himself as your
God, and everything else you need.

God is singing about you with a heart bursting
with joy and pride. He is your loving father. Listen
to the special song he is singing just for you!

God's Words of Life on

JOY

Our mouths were filled with laughter,
our tongues with songs of joy.
Then it was said among the nations,
"The LORD has done great things for them."
The LORD has done great things for us,
and we are filled with joy.

✿ PSALM 126:2-3

The LORD is my strength and my shield;
my heart trusts in him, and I am helped.
My heart leaps for joy
and I will give thanks to him in song.

✿ PSALM 28:7

Those living far away fear your wonders, O LORD;
where morning dawns and evening fades
you call forth songs of joy.

✿ PSALM 65:8

Light is shed upon the righteous
and joy on the upright in heart.

✿ PSALM 97:11

God's Words of Life on

JOY

Jesus said, "As the Father has loved me, so have I loved you. Now remain in my love. If you obey my commands, you will remain in my love, just as I have obeyed my Father's commands and remain in his love. I have told you this so that my joy may be in you and that your joy may be complete."

✿ **JOHN 15:9-11**

Satisfy us in the morning with your unfailing love, LORD,
that we may sing for joy and be glad all our days.

✿ **PSALM 90:14**

Only the redeemed will walk there,
the ransomed of the LORD will return.
They will enter Zion with singing;
everlasting joy will crown their heads.
Gladness and joy will overtake them,
and sorrow and sighing will flee away.

✿ **ISAIAH 35:9-10**

A cheerful look brings joy to the heart,
and good news gives health to the bones.

✿ **PROVERBS 15:30**

God's Words of Life on

May the God of hope fill you with all joy and peace as you trust in him, so that you may overflow with hope by the power of the Holy Spirit.

✿ ROMANS 15:13

You have made known to me the path of life, O LORD; you will fill me with joy in your presence, with eternal pleasures at your right hand.

✿ PSALM 16:11

Let all who take refuge in you be glad; let them ever sing for joy. Spread your protection over them, that those who love your name may rejoice in you. For surely, O LORD, you bless the righteous; you surround them with your favor as with a shield.

✿ PSALM 5:11-12

Jesus said, "Until now you have not asked for anything in my name. Ask and you will receive, and your joy will be complete."

✿ JOHN 16:24

God's Words of Life on

JOY

When I said, "My foot is slipping,"
your love, O LORD, supported me.
When anxiety was great within me,
your consolation brought joy to my soul.

✿ PSALM 94:18-19

The joy of the LORD is your strength.

✿ NEHEMIAH 8:10

Though you have not seen Jesus, you love him; and
even though you do not see him now, you believe in
him and are filled with an inexpressible and glorious
joy, for you are receiving the goal of your faith, the
salvation of
your souls.

✿ 1 PETER 1:8-9

Weeping may remain for a night,
but rejoicing comes in the morning.

✿ PSALM 30:5

God's Words of Life on

Joy

When your words came, I ate them;
*   they were my joy and my heart's delight,*
for I bear your name,
*   O LORD God Almighty.*

✿ JEREMIAH 15:16

You will go out in joy
*   and be led forth in peace;*
the mountains and hills
*   will burst into song before you,*
and all the trees of the field
*   will clap their hands.*

✿ ISAIAH 55:12

To God who is able to keep you from falling and to
present you before his glorious presence without fault
and with great joy—to the only God our Savior be
glory, majesty, power and authority, through Jesus
Christ our Lord, before all ages, now and forever-
more! Amen.

✿ JUDE 24-25

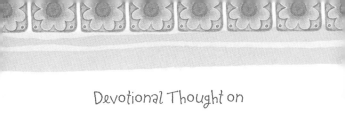

Devotional Thought on

JOY

JOY, NO MATTER WHAT

A Christian's joy is in God and in his promises. God is good, and God is faithful—no matter what is happening to you. That means that even on a day when you get a bad grade or have a stomachache or when your big Saturday picnic gets rained out, you can still feel okay deep down inside because you know God is taking care of you.

Read 1 Chronicles 16:8-12, 23-26. David wrote this psalm of praise to show the joy God's people have because of all that God does. You do not need to worry or be afraid. Even in difficult times you can go to God for strength.

If you are wanting joy in your life, ask God to fill you with his Holy Spirit. The Spirit is the joy-giver. "Ask and you will receive, and your joy will be complete" (John 16:24). That is a promise from Jesus' own lips, and he is faithful!

God's Words of Life on

Listening

I will listen to what God the LORD will say;
he promises peace to his people, his saints.

✿ **PSALM 85:8**

Jesus said, "The seed on good soil stands for those
with a noble and good heart, who hear the word,
retain it, and by persevering produce a crop."

✿ **LUKE 8:15**

He who listens to a life-giving rebuke
will be at home among the wise.

✿ **PROVERBS 15:31**

Pay attention and listen to the sayings of the wise;
apply your heart to what I teach,
for it is pleasing when you keep them in your heart
and have all of them ready on your lips.
So that your trust may be in the LORD,
I teach you today, even you.

✿ **PROVERBS 22:17-19**

God's Words of Life on

Listening

Jesus said, "Everyone who listens to the Father and learns from him comes to me."

✿ JOHN 6:45

The Sovereign LORD has given me an instructed tongue,
    to know the word that sustains the weary.
He wakens me morning by morning,
    wakens my ear to listen like one being taught.

✿ ISAIAH 50:4

Anyone who listens to the word but does not do what it says is like a man who looks at his face in a mirror and, after looking at himself, goes away and immediately forgets what he looks like. But the man who looks intently into the perfect law that gives freedom, and continues to do this, not forgetting what he has heard, but doing it—he will be blessed in what he does.

✿ JAMES 1:23-25

God's Words of Life on

Listening

Jesus said, "My sheep listen to my voice; I know them, and they follow me. I give them eternal life, and they shall never perish; no one can snatch them out of my hand. My Father, who has given them to me, is greater than all; no one can snatch them out of my Father's hand. I and the Father are one."

✿ JOHN 10:27-30

Let the wise listen and add to their learning.

✿ PROVERBS 1:5

*Listen to advice and accept instruction,
    and in the end you will be wise.*

✿ PROVERBS 19:20

Devotional Thought on

Listening

GOD'S VOICE

Can you imagine actually hearing the voice of God? Moses did. The Bible says over 100 times that God spoke to Moses! God wasn't silent then, and he's not silent today. Even though he doesn't usually speak out loud, God still talks to us.

If you believe in Jesus, he has given you his Holy Spirit. The Holy Spirit's job is to teach you about the Lord Jesus and to remind you of the things Jesus said in his Word, the Bible. The Bible is the main way the Holy Spirit speaks to his people today.

God is a person. He wants to be friends with you. A good friendship means that friends have to talk to each other and listen to each other. You talk to God when you pray. He talks to you when you read the Bible.

What should you do if you think God is telling you to do something? Always test a feeling to see if it agrees with the Bible. God will not say one thing in the Bible and the opposite thing in some other way.

You hear people say, "What would Jesus do?" That's not a bad way to think—if you read the Bible so you know what Jesus really would do. If you listen to the Holy Spirit through reading God's Word, you'll never go wrong.

God's Words of Life on

Love

Love is patient, love is kind. It does not envy, it does not boast, it is not proud. It is not rude, it is not self-seeking. It is not easily angered, it keeps no record of wrongs. Love does not delight in evil but rejoices with the truth. It always protects, always trusts, always hopes, always perseveres. Love never fails.

✿ 1 CORINTHIANS 13:4-8

*The LORD loves righteousness and justice;
    the earth is full of his unfailing love.*

✿ PSALM 33:5

God so loved the world that he gave his one and only Son, that whoever believes in him shall not perish but have eternal life.

✿ JOHN 3:16

How great is the love the Father has lavished on us, that we should be called children of God! And that is what we are!

✿ 1 JOHN 3:1

God's Words of Life on

Love

As God's chosen people, holy and dearly loved, clothe yourselves with compassion, kindness, humility, gentleness and patience. Bear with each other and forgive whatever grievances you may have against one another. Forgive as the Lord forgave you. And over all these virtues put on love, which binds them all together in perfect unity.

❀ COLOSSIANS 3:12-14

We know and rely on the love God has for us. God is love. Whoever lives in love lives in God, and God in him.

❀ 1 JOHN 4:16

I will praise you, O LORD, among the nations;
*   I will sing of you among the peoples.*
For great is your love, reaching to the heavens;
*   your faithfulness reaches to the skies.*

❀ PSALM 57:9-10

He who covers over an offense promotes love.

❀ PROVERBS 17:9

God's Words of Life on

Love

God has poured out his love into our hearts by the Holy Spirit, whom he has given us. ... God demonstrates his own love for us in this: While we were still sinners, Christ died for us.

✿ ROMANS 5:5, 8

Dear friends, let us love one another, for love comes from God. Everyone who loves has been born of God and knows God.

✿ 1 JOHN 4:7

*I trust in your unfailing love, O LORD;
    my heart rejoices in your salvation.
I will sing to the LORD,
    for he has been good to me.*

✿ PSALM 13:5-6

Greater love has no one than this, that he lay down his life for his friend.

✿ JOHN 15:13

God's Words of Life on

Love

Because of the LORD's great love we are not consumed,
for his compassions never fail.
They are new every morning;
great is your faithfulness.

✿ **LAMENTATIONS 3:22-23**

There is no fear in love. But perfect love drives
out fear.

✿ **1 JOHN 4:18**

I pray that you, being rooted and established in love,
may have power, together with all the saints, to
grasp how wide and long and high and deep is the
love of Christ, and to know this love that surpasses
knowledge—that you may be filled to the measure
of all the fullness of God.

✿ **EPHESIANS 3:17-19**

Jesus said, "Love one another. As I have loved you,
so you must love one another. By this all men will
know that you are my disciples, if you love one
another."

✿ **JOHN 13:34-35**

God's Words of Life on

Love

We love because God first loved us.

❀ 1 JOHN 4:19

This is love: not that we loved God, but that he loved us and sent his Son as an atoning sacrifice for our sins.

❀ 1 JOHN 4:10

God did not give us a spirit of timidity, but a spirit of power, of love and of self-discipline.

❀ 2 TIMOTHY 1:7

Those who plan what is good find love and faithfulness.

❀ PROVERBS 14:22

The LORD is gracious and compassionate,
  slow to anger and rich in love.
The LORD is good to all;
  he has compassion on all he has made.

❀ PSALM 145:8-9

Devotional Thought on

Love

GOD'S RIVER OF DELIGHTS

In Psalm 36:8, David uses a river as a metaphor for all the good things God gives. He calls this river the "river of delights." One thing that is flowing in this river of delights is God's love (Psalm 36:5). God's love is as high as the sky; it can't be bought and it never stops flowing (Psalm 36:7).

Ezekiel the prophet describes a river, too. Where Ezekiel starts into the water, it is only ankle-deep. Then it becomes knee-deep, then waist-deep, then deep enough to swim in—"a river that no one could cross" (Ezekiel 47:5).

We can think of getting to know God as something like this. When you begin to get to know God, you start slowly; you see his greatness. As you trust in God and your desire for more of him increases, he leads you deeper—that is, you get to know him better and better, like a best friend.

As you pray this week, think about God's love for you. Step into his river of delights, even if only up to your ankles. When you delight in God, he delights in you (Psalm 147:11).

God's Words of Life on

Money

I know what it is to be in need, and I know what it is to have plenty. I have learned the secret of being content in any and every situation, whether well fed or hungry, whether living in plenty or in want. I can do everything through Christ who gives me strength.

✿ **PHILIPPIANS 4:12-13**

He who gathers money little by little makes it grow.

✿ **PROVERBS 13:11**

Jesus sat down opposite the place where the offerings were put and watched the crowd putting their money into the temple treasury. Many rich people threw in large amounts. But a poor widow came and put in two very small copper coins, worth only a fraction of a penny. Calling his disciples to him, Jesus said, "I tell you the truth, this poor widow has put more into the treasury than all the others. They all gave out of their wealth; but she, out of her poverty, put in everything—all she had to live on."

✿ **MARK 12:41-44**

God's Words of Life on

Money

Wisdom is a shelter
as money is a shelter,
but the advantage of knowledge is this:
that wisdom preserves the life of its possessor.

✿ ECCLESIASTES 7:12

Keep your lives free from the love of money and be
content with what you have, because God has said,
"Never will I leave you;
never will I forsake you."
So we say with confidence,
"The Lord is my helper; I will not be afraid.
What can man do to me?"

✿ HEBREWS 13:5-6

Remember this: Whoever sows sparingly will also
reap sparingly, and whoever sows generously will
also reap generously. Each man should give what he
has decided in his heart to give, not reluctantly or
under compulsion, for God loves a cheerful giver.
And God is able to make all grace abound to you, so
that in all things at all times, having all that you
need, you will abound in every
good work.

✿ 2 CORINTHIANS 9:6-8

God's Words of Life on

Money

It is more blessed to give than to receive.

✿ ACTS 20:35

God who supplies seed to the sower and bread for food will also supply and increase your store of seed and will enlarge the harvest of your righteousness. You will be made rich in every way so that you can be generous on every occasion, and ... your generosity will result in thanksgiving to God.

✿ 2 CORINTHIANS 9:10-11

Good will come to him who is generous and lends freely,
 who conducts his affairs with justice.

✿ PSALM 112:5

"Bring the whole tithe into the storehouse, that there may be food in my house. Test me in this," says the LORD Almighty, "and see if I will not throw open the floodgates of heaven and pour out so much blessing that you will not have room enough for it."

✿ MALACHI 3:10

Devotional Thought on

Money

GIVING FROM YOUR HEART

What do you think you would do if your family was down the last $1.00 you had? How would you spend it?

In Mark 12:41-44 we read that Jesus watched the temple crowd as people gave their money. He heard the coins drop into the collection bin. The rich people gave lots of money, and Jesus nodded. It was good that they shared their wealth. Then he saw a poor widow. She gave two coins, worth less than a penny. Yet giving this much money was a true sacrifice for this woman. It was all the money she had—it would have bought her a little food to eat. In those days there wasn't the help for people that there is today—she didn't have a welfare check coming or food stamps. But she had faith that *God* would give her the food, clothes and place to live that she needed. Jesus saw her heart. And he sees your heart, too. Whatever you give from the *heart* is always big in the eyes of your Father.

God's Words of Life on

Obedience

This is love for God: to obey his commands. And his commands are not burdensome, for everyone born of God overcomes the world.

✿ 1 JOHN 5:3-4

I will always obey your law, LORD,
    for ever and ever.
I will walk about in freedom,
    for I have sought out your precepts.

✿ PSALM 119:44-45

Jesus said, "As the Father has loved me, so have I loved you. Now remain in my love. If you obey my commands, you will remain in my love, just as I have obeyed my Father's commands and remain in his love. I have told you this so that my joy may be in you and that your joy may be complete."

✿ JOHN 15:9-11

God's Words of Life on

Obedience

Children, obey your parents in the Lord, for this is right. "Honor your father and mother"—which is the first commandment with a promise—"that it may go well with you and that you may enjoy long life on the earth."

✿ EPHESIANS 6:1-3

He who obeys instructions guards his life.

✿ PROVERBS 19:16

Jesus said, "If anyone loves me, he will obey my teaching. My Father will love him, and we will come to him and make our home with him."

✿ JOHN 14:23

*Your statutes are wonderful, LORD;
     therefore I obey them.
The unfolding of your words gives light;
     it gives understanding to the simple.*

✿ PSALM 119:129-130

God's Words of Life on

Obedience

If anyone obeys his word, God's love is truly made complete in him.

❁ 1 JOHN 2:5

From everlasting to everlasting
the LORD's love is with those who fear him,
and his righteousness with their
children's children—
with those who keep his covenant
and remember to obey his precepts.

❁ PSALM 103:17-18

All these blessings will come upon you and accompany you if you obey the LORD your God: You will be blessed in the city and blessed in the country. The fruit of your womb will be blessed, and the crops of your land and the young of your livestock—the calves of your herds and the lambs of your flocks. Your basket and your kneading trough will be blessed. You will be blessed when you come in and blessed when you go out.

❁ DEUTERONOMY 28:2-6

Devotional Thought on

Obedience

WHOSE SLAVE ARE YOU?

We don't think of ourselves as slaves, do we? A slave obeys someone—or something. Even though you obey your parents, that's different than being a slave. Parents usually have their children's good in mind and want them to obey so that they will be safe and grow and mature and be on their own someday. A slave obeys for the good of the one he or she obeys. But the apostle Paul says all of us are slaves—either we obey sin or we obey what's right (Romans 6:16-18).

In Romans 8:9-17 we can read some wonderful news for those who believe in Jesus. Although you were once a slave controlled by sin, you are now free to be controlled by the Holy Spirit. And God has declared that you are his child (1 John 3:1)! You now have the freedom to serve and obey God (Ephesians 6:6) and to serve other Christians in love (Galatians 5:13).

The freedom described in the Bible is not freedom to be independent. You will always have to obey a master. If you choose to obey God, it will lead to eternal life (Romans 6:16, 22)!

Ask God to show you the areas in your life that need his help. Pray for the Holy Spirit's power to choose God's way and God's will in your life. When you obey him you will find true freedom to enjoy both God and your life.

God's Words of Life on

Patience

Be patient, ... until the Lord's coming. See how the farmer waits for the land to yield its valuable crop and how patient he is for the autumn and spring rains. Be patient and stand firm, because the Lord's coming is near.

✿ JAMES 5:7-8

Love is patient.

✿ 1 CORINTHIANS 13:4

I waited patiently for the LORD;
*   he turned to me and heard my cry.*

✿ PSALM 40:1

The Lord is not slow in keeping his promise, as some understand slowness. He is patient with you, not wanting anyone to perish, but everyone to come to repentance.

✿ 2 PETER 3:9

A man's wisdom gives him patience;
*   it is to his glory to overlook an offense.*

✿ PROVERBS 19:11

God's Words of Life on

Patience

The end of a matter is better than its beginning, and patience is better than pride.

✿ ECCLESIASTES 7:8

A patient man has great understanding.

✿ PROVERBS 14:29

Be joyful in hope, patient in affliction, faithful in prayer.

✿ ROMANS 12:12

The fruit of the Spirit is love, joy, peace, patience, kindness, goodness, faithfulness, gentleness and self-control.

✿ GALATIANS 5:22-23

Be completely humble and gentle; be patient, bearing with one another in love. Make every effort to keep the unity of the Spirit through the bond of peace.

✿ EPHESIANS 4:2-3

God's Words of Life on

Patience

We pray ... that you may live a life worthy of the Lord and may please him in every way: bearing fruit in every good work, growing in the knowledge of God, being strengthened with all power according to his glorious might so that you may have great endurance and patience, and joyfully giving thanks to the Father.

✿ COLOSSIANS 1:10-12

As God's chosen people, holy and dearly loved, clothe yourselves with compassion, kindness, humility, gentleness and patience.

✿ COLOSSIANS 3:12

Bear in mind that our Lord's patience means salvation.

✿ 2 PETER 3:15

Jesus said, "Since you have kept my command to endure patiently, I will also keep you from the hour of trial that is going to come upon the whole world to test those who live on the earth."

✿ REVELATION 3:10

Devotional Thought on

Patience

GOD IS PATIENT

Do you like science fiction stories? How about when the character travels in time? It's hard to think about, but try to imagine you are outside of time, like God. To God, time doesn't matter the way it does to us. We feel rushed sometimes, but God never feels rushed. We feel like time drags, especially that last hour before school gets out. But time never drags for God.

Christians have been waiting for two thousand years for Christ to come back. That seems like a long time to us—but not to God. He is patient because he wants everyone to have a chance to believe in Jesus. But one day, Jesus *will* come.

If God is this lovingly patient with people who don't believe in him, then we can be patient with little brothers or sisters who irritate us or that teacher who keeps teaching even after the bell rings. By being patient with people and situations in your life, you are following God's perfect example.

God's Words of Life on

Peace

Jesus said, "Peace I leave with you; my peace I give you. I do not give to you as the world gives. Do not let your hearts be troubled and do not be afraid."

✿ JOHN 14:27

To us a child is born,
to us a son is given,
and the government will be on his shoulders.
And he will be called
Wonderful Counselor, Mighty God,
Everlasting Father, Prince of Peace.

✿ ISAIAH 9:6

The LORD gives strength to his people;
the LORD blesses his people with peace.

✿ PSALM 29:11

You will keep in perfect peace
him whose mind is steadfast,
because he trusts in you, O LORD.

✿ ISAIAH 26:3

God's Words of Life on

Peace

Be still, and know that I am God.

✿ PSALM 46:10

The fruit of righteousness will be peace;
*   the effect of righteousness will be quietness and*
confidence forever.

✿ ISAIAH 32:17

Let the peace of Christ rule in your hearts, since as
members of one body you were called to peace. And
be thankful.

✿ COLOSSIANS 3:15

Great peace have they who love your law, O LORD,
*   and nothing can make them stumble.*

✿ PSALM 119:165

God's Words of Life on

Peace

Consider the blameless, observe the upright;
*   there is a future for the man of peace.*

✿ PSALM 37:37

How beautiful on the mountains
*   are the feet of those who bring good news,*
who proclaim peace,
*   who bring good tidings,*
*   who proclaim salvation,*
who say to Zion,
*   "Your God reigns!"*

✿ ISAIAH 52:7

I will listen to what God the LORD will say;
*   he promises peace to his people, his saints.*

✿ PSALM 85:8

Those who walk uprightly
*   enter into peace.*

✿ ISAIAH 57:2

God's Words of Life on

Peace

*"Though the mountains be shaken
and the hills be removed,
yet my unfailing love for you will not be shaken
nor my covenant of peace be removed,"
says the LORD, who has compassion on you.*

✿ ISAIAH 54:10

*LORD , you establish peace for us;
all that we have accomplished
you have done for us.*

✿ ISAIAH 26:12

A heart at peace gives life to the body.

✿ PROVERBS 14:30

*Grace, mercy and peace from God the Father and
from Jesus Christ, the Father's Son, will be with us in
truth and love.*

✿ 2 JOHN 1:3

God's Words of Life on

Peace

May the Lord of peace himself give you peace at all times and in every way.

✿ 2 THESSALONIANS 3:16

May God himself, the God of peace, sanctify you through and through. May your whole spirit, soul and body be kept blameless at the coming of our Lord Jesus Christ.

✿ 1 THESSALONIANS 5:23

In Christ Jesus you who once were far away have been brought near through the blood of Christ. For he himself is our peace.

✿ EPHESIANS 2:13-14

The mind controlled by the Spirit is life and peace.

✿ ROMANS 8:6

Since we have been justified through faith, we have peace with God through our Lord Jesus Christ.

✿ ROMANS 5:1

Devotional Thought on

Peace

JESUS, THE PRINCE OF PEACE

What does the word peace make you think of? Countries getting along instead of fighting wars? People getting along instead of fighting and arguing? Getting along with God? Peace can mean all these things. It can also mean a feeling of quiet deep down inside of you; a quietness that doesn't leave you, even when things in your life go wrong.

Would you like to have that kind of peace in your soul? If you love Jesus and believe in him he will give you peace because he is called the Prince of Peace! Spend time talking to Jesus every day and reading his words in the Bible. The more time you spend getting to know Jesus, the more of his peace you will feel in your heart. Then, if bad things happen, you can still have peace knowing that Jesus is your friend and that he will always be with you and will always help you. That's a great reason to feel at peace!

God's Words of Life on

Perseverance

You need to persevere so that when you have done the will of God, you will receive what he has promised.

✿ HEBREWS 10:36

The testing of your faith develops perseverance. Perseverance must finish its work so that you may be mature and complete, not lacking anything.

✿ JAMES 1:3-4

Love always protects, always trusts, always hopes, always perseveres.

✿ 1 CORINTHIANS 13:7

Blessed is the man who perseveres under trial, because when he has stood the test, he will receive the crown of life that God has promised to those who love him.

✿ JAMES 1:12

God's Words of Life on

Perseverance

Since we are surrounded by such a great cloud of witnesses, let us throw off everything that hinders and the sin that so easily entangles, and let us run with perseverance the race marked out for us. Let us fix our eyes on Jesus, the author and perfecter of our faith, who for the joy set before him endured the cross, scorning its shame, and sat down at the right hand of the throne of God. Consider him who endured such opposition from sinful men, so that you will not grow weary and lose heart.

✿ HEBREWS 12:1-3

We consider blessed those who have persevered. You have heard of Job's perseverance and have seen what the Lord finally brought about. The Lord is full of compassion and mercy.

✿ JAMES 5:11

Let us not become weary in doing good, for at the proper time we will reap a harvest if we do not give up.

✿ GALATIANS 6:9

God's Words of Life on

Perseverance

Make every effort to add to your faith goodness; and to goodness, knowledge; and to knowledge, self-control; and to self-control, perseverance; and to perseverance, godliness; and to godliness, brotherly kindness; and to brotherly kindness, love. For if you possess these qualities in increasing measure, they will keep you from being ineffective and unproductive in your knowledge of our Lord Jesus Christ.

✿ 2 PETER 1:5-8

We also rejoice in our sufferings, because we know that suffering produces perseverance; perseverance, character; and character, hope.

✿ ROMANS 5:3-4

May the Lord direct your hearts into God's love and Christ's perseverance.

✿ 2 THESSALONIANS 3:5

Devotional Thought on

Perseverance

TROUBLES BRING PERSEVERANCE

People look lots of places for the good things that only God gives: peace, joy, love, and heaven. But God wants people to look for him, not just for the good things he gives. And when people love and trust God, they can even rejoice in their troubles, because they know God is doing good things for them and for others through their troubles.

Romans 5:3 says that troubles produce "perseverance." Do you play any sports? Then you know something about perseverance. You practice and prepare in order to build up your strength and endurance so you don't quit a race or a game in the middle. You can keep going to the end, even though it's hard. In the same way, troubles can cause you to get stronger in your faith.

So no matter what you're going through, keep looking for the good that God wants to bring you through your troubles. He is helping you develop strength and perseverance so you can make it through anything—with God by your side!

God's Words of Life on

Prayer

The Spirit helps us in our weakness. We do not know what we ought to pray for, but the Spirit himself intercedes for us with groans that words cannot express.

✿ ROMANS 8:26

Hear my prayer, O LORD;
*   listen to my cry for mercy.*
In the day of my trouble I will call to you
*   for you will answer me.*

✿ PSALM 86:6-7

"Call to me and I will answer you and tell you great and unsearchable things you do not know," says the LORD.

✿ JEREMIAH 33:3

"When you pray go into your room, close the door and pray to your Father, who is unseen. Then your Father, who sees what is done in secret, will reward you."

✿ MATTHEW 6:6

God's Words of Life on

Prayer

The prayer offered in faith will make the sick person well; the Lord will raise him up. If he has sinned, he will be forgiven. Therefore confess your sins to each other and pray for each other so that you may be healed. The prayer of a righteous man is powerful and effective.

✿ **JAMES 5:15-16**

The eyes of the Lord are on the righteous and his ears are attentive to their prayer.

✿ **1 PETER 3:12**

Know that the LORD has set apart the godly for himself;
    The LORD will hear when I call to him.

✿ **PSALM 4:3**

I called on your name, O LORD,
    from the depths of the pit.
You heard my plea: "Do not close your ears
    to my cry for relief."
You came near when I called you,
    and you said, "Do not fear."

✿ **LAMENTATIONS 3:55-57**

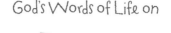

God's Words of Life on

Prayer

I urge ... that requests, prayers, intercession and thanksgiving be made for everyone—for kings and all those in authority, that we may live peaceful and quiet lives in all godliness and holiness.

✿ 1 TIMOTHY 2:1-2

O LORD, I call to you; come quickly to me.
   Hear my voice when I call to you.
May my prayer be set before you like incense;
   May the lifting up of my hands
be like the evening sacrifice.

✿ PSALM 141:1-2

This is the confidence we have in approaching God: that if we ask anything according to his will, he hears us. And if we know that he hears us—whatever we ask—we know that we have what we asked of him.

✿ 1 JOHN 5:14-15

If any of you lacks wisdom, he should ask God, who gives generously to all without finding fault, and it will be given to him.

✿ JAMES 1:5

God's Words of Life on

Prayer

Do not be anxious about anything, but in everything, by prayer and petition, with thanksgiving, present your requests to God. And the peace of God, which transcends all understanding, will guard your hearts and your minds in Christ Jesus.

✿ PHILIPPIANS 4:6-7

Listen to my cry for help,
my King and my God,
for to you I pray.
In the morning, O LORD, you hear my voice;
in the morning I lay my requests before you
and wait in expectation.

✿ PSALM 5:2-3

Let everyone who is godly pray to you, LORD,
while you may be found;
surely when the mighty waters rise,
they will not reach him.

✿ PSALM 32:6

God's Words of Life on

Prayer

God has surely listened
    and heard my voice in prayer.
Praise be to God,
    who has not rejected my prayer
    or withheld his love from me!

✿ PSALM 66:19-20

Jesus said, "This, then, is how you should pray:
'Our Father in heaven,
hallowed be your name,
your kingdom come,
your will be done
    on earth as it is in heaven.
Give us today our daily bread.
Forgive us our debts,
    as we also have forgiven our debtors.
And lead us not into temptation,
but deliver us from the evil one.'"

✿ MATTHEW 6:9-13

In my distress I called to the LORD,
    and he answered me.

✿ JONAH 2:2

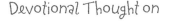

Devotional Thought on

Prayer

GOD, HELP ME
TO UNDERSTAND PRAYER

The Bible teaches a lot about prayer, like where and when we should pray, what and who we should pray for, and who helps us pray.

Romans 8:26-27 says that we get help when we pray. Think of a time when you felt you couldn't describe what you were feeling in your heart. If you believe in Jesus, the Holy Spirit will help you express your heart to God.

In Matthew 14:23 and Mark 1:35 it says that Jesus prayed long into the night. Other times he woke up long before anyone else in order to pray. That's how important he thought prayer is.

No matter who you are you can pray to God and if you believe in Jesus, he will hear you every time. God hears and answers the prayers of people who believe in Jesus because Jesus paid for their sins.

If you aren't sure what to pray, you can use this as your prayer: *Dear God, thank you for listening to me. Help me to pray to you a lot. Help me to remember that you are always here for me and that you love me. Amen.*

God's Words of Life on

Protection

Jesus prayed, "I pray for [my disciples]. I am not praying for the world, but for those you have given me, for they are yours. All I have is yours, and all you have is mine. And glory has come to me through them. I will remain in the world no longer, but they are still in the world, and I am coming to you. Holy Father, protect them by the power of your name— the name you gave me—so that they may be one as we are one."

✿ JOHN 17:9-11

Do not forsake wisdom, and she will protect you; love her, and she will watch over you.

✿ PROVERBS 4:6

Let all who take refuge in you be glad, O LORD; let them ever sing for joy.
Spread your protection over them, that those who love your name may rejoice in you.

✿ PSALM 5:11

God's Words of Life on

Protection

"Because he loves me," says the LORD, *"I will rescue him;*
I will protect him, for he acknowledges my name.
He will call upon me, and I will answer him;
I will be with him in trouble,
I will deliver him and honor him.
With long life will I satisfy him
and show him my salvation."

✿ PSALM 91:14-16

You are my hiding place, LORD;
you will protect me from trouble
and surround me with songs of deliverance.

✿ PSALM 32:7

Show the wonder of your great love, LORD,
you who save by your right hand
those who take refuge in you from their foes.
Keep me as the apple of your eye;
hide me in the shadow of your wings.

✿ PSALM 17:7-8

149

God's Words of Life on

Protection

The LORD gives wisdom,
        and from his mouth come
        knowledge and understanding.
He holds victory in store for the upright,
        he is a shield to those whose walk is blameless,
for he guards the course of the just
        and protects the way of his faithful ones.

✿ PROVERBS 2:6-8

My help comes from the LORD,
        the Maker of heaven and earth.
He will not let your foot slip—
        he who watches over you will not slumber;
indeed, he who watches over Israel
        will neither slumber nor sleep.
The LORD watches over you—
        the LORD is your shade at your right hand;
the sun will not harm you by day,
        nor the moon by night.
The LORD will keep you from all harm—
        he will watch over your life;
the LORD will watch over your coming and going
        both now and forevermore.

✿ PSALM 121:2-8

God's Words of Life on

Protection

He who dwells in the shelter of the Most High
*   will rest in the shadow of the Almighty.*
I will say of the LORD, "He is my refuge and my fortress,
*   my God, in whom I trust." ...*
He will cover you with his feathers,
*   and under his wings you will find refuge;*
*   his faithfulness will be your shield and rampart.*
You will not fear the terror of night,
*   nor the arrow that flies by day,*
nor the pestilence that stalks in the darkness,
*   nor the plague that destroys at midday.*
A thousand may fall at your side,
*   ten thousand at your right hand,*
*   but it will not come near you. ...*
If you make the Most High your dwelling—
*   even the LORD, who is my refuge—*
then no harm will befall you,
*   no disaster will come near your tent.*
For he will command his angels concerning you
*   to guard you in all your ways;*
they will lift you up in their hands,
*   so that you will not strike your foot against a stone.*

❀ **PSALM 91:1-2, 4-7, 9-12**

Do not withhold your mercy from me, O LORD;
*   may your love and your truth always protect me.*
❀ **PSALM 40:11**

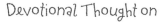

Devotional Thought on

Protection

GOD'S GEAR

In Ephesians 6:10-18 we read that God has given Christians armor to protect them. Here are the pieces of God's full armor:

✿ **The Belt of Truth**—You believe the truth (God's Word) and you tell the truth. God's Word helps you to see the difference between truth and lies (Ephesians 1:13).

✿ **The Breastplate of Righteousness**—If you are a Christian, God counts Jesus Christ's goodness, or righteousness, as yours (2 Corinthians 5:21).

✿ **The Shoes of the Gospel of Peace**—The gospel of peace is all that God did to make peace between him and us by sending Jesus to die for our sins.

✿ **The Shield of Faith**—Your trust in Jesus, no matter what, protects you from your enemy (Hebrews 10:22).

Devotional Thought on

Protection

- ✿ **The Helmet of Salvation**—"Salvation" means Jesus saves you by his suffering and dying.
- ✿ **The Sword of the Spirt**—When you memorize Bible verses and say them or read them out loud, you are making the enemy listen to God and not to you, because the Bible is God's Word.

Soldiers have to get all their gear together before they go out to fight. In the same way, a Christian must put on God's gear, or armor, before every day's battle. Memorize Scripture. Pray the words of Scripture. And always remember that God is protecting you through every battle!

I am with you and will watch over you wherever you go... I will not leave you until I have done what I have promised you.
✿ **Genesis 28:15**

God's Words of Life on

Rest

Jesus said, "Come to me, all you who are weary and burdened, and I will give you rest. Take my yoke upon you and learn from me, for I am gentle and humble in heart, and you will find rest for your souls. For my yoke is easy and my burden is light."

✿ **MATTHEW 11:28-30**

I will lie down and sleep in peace,
for you alone, O LORD,
make me dwell in safety.

✿ **PSALM 4:8**

The LORD is gracious and righteous;
our God is full of compassion.
The LORD protects the simplehearted;
when I was in great need, he saved me.
Be at rest once more, O my soul,
for the LORD has been good to you.

✿ **PSALM 116:5-7**

My soul finds rest in God alone;
my salvation comes from him.

✿ **PSALM 62:1**

God's Words of Life on

Rest

Let the beloved of the LORD rest secure in him,
for he shields him all day long,
and the one the LORD loves rests
between his shoulders.

✿ DEUTERONOMY 33:12

I have set the LORD always before me.
Because he is at my right hand,
I will not be shaken.
Therefore my heart is glad and my tongue rejoices;
my body also will rest secure.

✿ PSALM 16:8-9

When you lie down, you will not be afraid;
When you lie down, your sleep will be sweet.

✿ PROVERBS 3:24

Ask where the good way is, and walk in it,
and you will find rest for your souls.

✿ JEREMIAH 6:16

God's Words of Life on

Rest

By the seventh day [of creation] God had finished the work he had been doing; so on the seventh day he rested from all his work. And God blessed the seventh day and made it holy, because on it he rested from all the work of creating that he had done.

✿ GENESIS 2:2-3

In repentance and rest is your salvation,
    in quietness and trust is your strength.

✿ ISAIAH 30:15

Then, because so many people were coming and going that they did not even have a chance to eat, Jesus said to [his disciples], "Come with me by your-selves to a quiet place and get some rest."

✿ MARK 6:31

He who dwells in the shelter of the Most High
    will rest in the shadow of the Almighty.

✿ PSALM 91:1

God's Words of Life on

Rest

Find rest, O my soul, in God alone;
my hope comes from him.

❁ **PSALM 62:5**

"My people will live in peaceful dwelling places,
in secure homes,
in undisturbed places of rest," says the LORD.

❁ **ISAIAH 32:18**

There remains, then, a Sabbath-rest for the people of
God; for anyone who enters God's rest also rests
from his own work, just as God did from his.

❁ **HEBREWS 4:9-10**

The fear of the LORD *leads to life:*
Then one rests content, untouched by trouble.

❁ **PROVERBS 19:23**

I lie down and sleep; I wake again,
because the LORD *sustains me.*

❁ **PSALM 3:5**

God's Words of Life on

Rest

God grants sleep to those he loves.

✿ **PSALM 127:2**

My heart is not proud, O LORD,
my eyes are not haughty;
I do not concern myself with great matters
or things too wonderful for me.
But I have stilled and quieted my soul;
like a weaned child with its mother,
like a weaned child is my soul within me.

✿ **PSALM 131:1-2**

You gave abundant showers, O God;
you refreshed your weary inheritance.

✿ **PSALM 68:9**

"I will refresh the weary and satisfy the faint," says
the LORD.

✿ **JEREMIAH 31:25**

Devotional Thought on

Rest

JESUS GIVES YOU REST

Do you ever feel stressed out? Do you have too much homework, too many after-school activities, or too many chores to finish? It is good to get your work done, but it is also important to rest sometimes and just be with God.

In Matthew 11:28-30 Jesus says, "Come to me, all you who are weary and burdened, and I will give you rest. Take my yoke upon you and learn from me, for I am gentle and humble in heart, and you will find rest for your souls. For my yoke is easy and my burden is light."

So what is a yoke? A yoke is a wooden frame put over the necks of two animals, like oxen or horses, so that they can work together. The experienced animal sets the speed they walk. The younger animal can't run ahead, fall behind or pull away because it is connected to the older one. Soon, the young animal learns from the more experienced one.

Jesus wants you to be yoked with him and learn from him. Instead of being burdened with worrying about doing everything with your own strength, you can let Jesus help you get things done. Jesus will help you with your worries and give you a break from all your concerns. You will find rest for your soul in him.

God's Words of Life on

Salvation

God so loved the world that he gave his one and only Son, that whoever believes in him shall not perish but have eternal life. For God did not send his Son into the world to condemn the world, but to save the world through him.

✿ JOHN 3:16-17

The LORD is my rock, my fortress and my deliverer;
    my God is my rock, in whom I take refuge.
He is my shield and the horn of my salvation,
    my stronghold.

✿ PSALM 18:2

Jesus said, "The Son of Man came to seek and to save what was lost."

✿ LUKE 19:10

Jesus said, "My Father's will is that everyone who looks to the Son and believes in him shall have eternal life, and I will raise him up at the last day."

✿ JOHN 6:40

God's Words of Life on

Salvation

I know that the LORD saves his anointed;
he answers him from his holy heaven
with the saving power of his right hand.
Some trust in chariots and some in horses,
but we trust in the name of the LORD our God.

✿ **PSALM 20:6-7**

Christ was sacrificed once to take away the sins of
many people; and he will appear a second time, not
to bear sin, but to bring salvation to those who are
waiting for him.

✿ **HEBREWS 9:28**

The LORD is the strength of his people,
a fortress of salvation for his anointed one.
Save your people and bless your inheritance;
be their shepherd and carry them forever.

✿ **PSALM 28:8-9**

Jesus is able to save completely those who come to
God through him, because he always lives to inter-
cede for them.

✿ **HEBREWS 7:25**

God's Words of Life on

Salvation

The grace of God that brings salvation has appeared to all men. It teaches us to say "No" to ungodliness and worldly passions, and to live self-controlled, upright and godly lives in this present age, while we wait for the blessed hope—the glorious appearing of our great God and Savior, Jesus Christ, who gave himself for us to redeem us from all wickedness and to purify for himself a people that are his very own, eager to do what is good.

✿ TITUS 2:11-14

*The salvation of the righteous comes from the LORD;
    he is their stronghold in time of trouble.*

✿ PSALM 37:39

If you confess with your mouth, "Jesus is Lord," and believe in your heart that God raised him from the dead, you will be saved.

✿ ROMANS 10:9

*The LORD takes delight in his people;
    he crowns the humble with salvation.*

✿ PSALM 149:4

God's Words of Life on

Salvation

The LORD is my strength and my song;
he has become my salvation.

✿ **PSALM 118:14**

Jesus said, "Whoever drinks the water I give him
will never thirst. Indeed, the water I give him will
become in him a spring of water welling up to eter-
nal life."

✿ **JOHN 4:14**

In him we were also chosen, having been predes-
tined according to the plan of him who works out
everything in conformity with the purpose of his
will, in order that we, who were the first to hope in
Christ, might be for the praise of his glory. And you
also were included in Christ when you heard the
word of truth, the gospel of your salvation. Having
believed, you were marked in him with a seal, the
promised Holy Spirit, who is a deposit guaranteeing
our inheritance until the redemption of those who
are God's possession—to the praise of his glory.

✿ **EPHESIANS 1:11-14**

God's Words of Life on

Salvation

Jesus said, "My sheep listen to my voice; I know them, and they follow me. I give them eternal life, and they shall never perish; no one can snatch them out of my hand."

✿ JOHN 10:27-28

Because of his great love for us, God, who is rich in mercy, made us alive with Christ even when we were dead in transgressions—it is by grace you have been saved. And God raised us up with Christ and seated us with him in the heavenly realms in Christ Jesus, in order that in the coming ages he might show the incomparable riches of his grace, expressed in his kindness to us in Christ Jesus. For it is by grace you have been saved, through faith—and this not from yourselves, it is the gift of God—not by works, so that no one can boast.

✿ EPHESIANS 2:4-9

I will give you thanks, for you answered me, O LORD; you have become my salvation.

✿ PSALM 118:21

God's Words of Life on

Salvation

Jesus said, "I tell you the truth, whoever hears my word and believes him who sent me has eternal life and will not be condemned; he has crossed over from death to life."

✿ JOHN 5:24

Jesus prayed, "Now this is eternal life: that they may know you, the only true God, and Jesus Christ, whom you have sent."

✿ JOHN 17:3

The wages of sin is death, but the gift of God is eternal life in Christ Jesus our Lord.

✿ ROMANS 6:23

Jesus said, "I am the resurrection and the life. He who believes in me will live, even though he dies; and whoever lives and believes in me will never die."

✿ JOHN 11:25-26

God's Words of Life on

Salvation

The LORD is my light and my salvation—
  whom shall I fear?
The LORD is the stronghold of my life—
  of whom shall I be afraid?

✿ PSALM 27:1

Jesus said, "I tell you the truth, he who believes has
everlasting life. I am the bread of life. ... Here is the
bread that comes down from heaven, which a man
may eat and not die. I am the living bread that came
down from heaven. If anyone eats of this bread, he
will live forever. This bread is my flesh, which I will
give for the life of the world."

✿ JOHN 6:47-48, 50-51

The LORD redeems his servants;
  no one will be condemned
who takes refuge in him.

✿ PSALM 34:22

Devotional Thought on

Salvation

YOU CAN BE FRIENDS
WITH GOD

In Exodus 25:10-22 we read about the tabernacle, where the Hebrew people worshiped God. The tabernacle was a big tent with three main parts: the Most Holy Place, the Holy Place and the courtyard. A curtain separated the Most Holy Place from the Holy Place, which was a larger room. Another curtain separated the Holy Place from the courtyard, the largest room of the tabernacle.

All the people could worship in the courtyard. Only the priests could go into the Holy Place. And only the high priest could go into the Most Holy Place, and he could only go in once a year to make a sacrifice. People couldn't be with God because God is holy and people are sinful. But today, because Jesus died on the cross for sins, everyone who believes in Jesus not only can be with God, but also has God living right in him or her!

God has made it so you can talk to him in person. That way is through believing in Jesus. Jesus' death for sin makes it possible for us to be friends with God and for God to be friends with us. Whenever you pray, remind yourself that you are talking to God and thank him for his gift of salvation through Jesus!

God's Words of Life on

Sharing the Good News

Jesus said, "Go and make disciples of all nations, baptizing them in the name of the Father and of the Son and of the Holy Spirit, and teaching them to obey everything I have commanded you. And surely I am with you always, to the very end of the age."

✿ MATTHEW 28:19-20

I urge ... that requests, prayers, intercession and thanksgiving be made for everyone—for kings and all those in authority, that we may live peaceful and quiet lives in all godliness and holiness. This is good, and pleases God our Savior, who wants all men to be saved and to come to a knowledge of the truth.

✿ 1 TIMOTHY 2:1-4

Thanks be to God, who always leads us in triumphal procession in Christ and through us spreads every-where the fragrance of the knowledge of him. For we are to God the aroma of Christ among those who are being saved and those who are perishing.

✿ 2 CORINTHIANS 2:14-15

God's Words of Life on

Sharing the Good News

All over the world this gospel is bearing fruit and growing.

✿ COLOSSIANS 1:6

I do not hide your righteousness in my heart, O LORD;
*   I speak of your faithfulness and salvation.*
I do not conceal your love and your truth
*   from the great assembly.*

✿ PSALM 40:10

If one of you should wander from the truth and someone should bring him back, remember this: Whoever turns a sinner from the error of his way will save him from death and cover over a multitude of sins.

✿ JAMES 5:19-20

God, who said, "Let light shine out of darkness," made his light shine in our hearts to give us the light of the knowledge of the glory of God in the face of Christ. But we have this treasure in jars of clay to show that this all-surpassing power is from God and not from us.

✿ 2 CORINTHIANS 4:6-7

God's Words of Life on

Sharing the Good News

I will declare your name to my brothers, LORD;
in the congregation I will praise you.

✿ **PSALM 22:22**

Though I am free and belong to no man, I make
myself a slave to everyone, to win as many as
possible. ... I have become all things to all men so
that by all possible means I might save some. I do
all this for the sake of the gospel, that I may share
in its blessings.

✿ **1 CORINTHIANS 9:19, 22-23**

My mouth will tell of your righteousness,
of your salvation all day long,
though I know not its measure.
I will come and proclaim your mighty acts,
O Sovereign LORD;
I will proclaim your righteousness, yours alone.

✿ **PSALM 71:15-16**

God's Words of Life on

Sharing the Good News

God did not give us a spirit of timidity, but a spirit of power, of love and of self-discipline. So do not be ashamed to testify about our Lord.

✿ 2 Timothy 1:7-8

How beautiful on the mountains
*   are the feet of those who bring good news,*
who proclaim peace,
*   who bring good tidings,*
*   who proclaim salvation,*
who say to Zion,
*   "Your God reigns!"*

✿ Isaiah 52:7

I try to please everybody in every way. For I am not seeking my own good but the good of many, so that they may be saved.

✿ 1 Corinthians 10:33

I am not ashamed of the gospel, because it is the power of God for the salvation of everyone who believes.

✿ Romans 1:16

God's Words of Life on

Sharing the Good News

Jesus said, "Whoever wants to save his life will lose it, but whoever loses his life for me and for the gospel will save it."

✿ MARK 8:35

This is the testimony: God has given us eternal life, and this life is in his Son.

✿ 1 JOHN 5:11

We know that we live in God and he in us, because he has given us of his Spirit. And we have seen and testify that the Father has sent his Son to be the Savior of the world. If anyone acknowledges that Jesus is the Son of God, God lives in him and he in God.

✿ 1 JOHN 4:13-15

Jesus said, "You will receive power when the Holy Spirit comes on you; and you will be my witnesses in Jerusalem, and in all Judea and Samaria, and to the ends of the earth."

✿ ACTS 1:8

Devotional Thought on

Sharing the Good News

A MEETING PLANNED BY GOD

God has a plan. In Acts 8:26-40 God tells Philip to go down the road, so Philip starts out, even though he has no idea what will happen next. He meets a government official from Ethiopia who has been to Jerusalem to worship and is on his way home. The Ethiopian is sitting in his chariot reading the Bible book of Isaiah. God is talking to him through the prophet Isaiah's words.

Philip stops and asks the official if he understands what he is reading. The man says, "I need someone to teach me." The official invites Philip to explain the Scripture he's reading. Philip explains the Good News about Jesus starting right there in Isaiah.

God works in people's hearts even when you don't know it. It's a Christian's job to tell people the truth about Jesus. God is the one who changes people's minds. Do you know people who might like to have God's Word explained to them?

Make a list of people you know who are not believers—friends and family members who might need to hear the Good News. Ask God to give you chances to tell these people about your faith. In the next few days and weeks, pray for the people on your list. See what happens and trust in God to change their hearts and minds.

God's Words of Life on

Strength

*Those who hope in the LORD
will renew their strength.
They will soar on wings like eagles;
they will run and not grow weary,
they will walk and not be faint.*

✿ ISAIAH 40:31

*Jesus said, "My grace is sufficient for you, for my
power is made perfect in weakness." Therefore I will
boast all the more gladly about my weaknesses, so
that Christ's power may rest on me.*

✿ 2 CORINTHIANS 12:9

*The LORD is my strength and my shield;
my heart trusts in him, and I am helped.
My heart leaps for joy
and I will give thanks to him in song.*

✿ PSALM 28:7

The joy of the LORD is your strength.

✿ NEHEMIAH 8:10

God's Words of Life on

Strength

God is our refuge and strength,
an ever-present help in trouble.
Therefore we will not fear, though the earth give way
and the mountains fall into the heart of the sea,
though its waters roar and foam
and the mountains quake with their surging.

✿ **PSALM 46:1-3**

I can do everything through Christ who gives me
strength.

✿ **PHILIPPIANS 4:13**

Surely God is my salvation;
I will trust and not be afraid.
The LORD, the LORD, is my strength and my song;
he has become my salvation.

✿ **ISAIAH 12:2**

The Lord stood at my side and gave me strength, so
that through me the message might be fully pro-
claimed.

✿ **2 TIMOTHY 4:17**

God's Words of Life on

Strength

The Lord said, "Do not fear, for I am with you;
*   do not be dismayed, for I am your God.*
I will strengthen you and help you;
*   I will uphold you with my righteous right hand."*

✿ ISAIAH 41:10

Be strong in the Lord and in his mighty power.

✿ EPHESIANS 6:10

The LORD gives strength to his people;
*   the LORD blesses his people with peace.*

✿ PSALM 29:11

I pray ... that you may know ... God's incomparably
great power for us who believe. That power is like
the working of his mighty strength, which he exerted
in Christ when he raised him from the dead and
seated him at his right hand in the heavenly realms.

✿ EPHESIANS 1:18-20

God's Words of Life on

Strength

Nothing is impossible with God.

✿ **LUKE 1:37**

*The LORD gives strength to the weary
    and increases the power of the weak.*

✿ **ISAIAH 40:29**

*The Sovereign LORD is my strength;
    he makes my feet like the feet of a deer,
    he enables me to go on the heights.*

✿ **HABAKKUK 3:19**

*One thing God has spoken,
    two things have I heard:
    that you, O God, are strong,
    and that you, O LORD, are loving.*

✿ **PSALM 62:11-12**

*O my Strength, I watch for you;
    you, O God, are my fortress, my loving God.*

✿ **PSALM 59:9-10**

God's Words of Life on

Strength

From the ends of the earth I call to you, LORD,
I call as my heart grows faint;
lead me to the rock that is higher than I.
For you have been my refuge,
a strong tower against the foe.

✿ **PSALM 61:2-3**

The God of all grace, who called you to his eternal
glory in Christ, after you have suffered a little while,
will himself restore you and make you strong, firm
and steadfast.

✿ **1 PETER 5:10**

Glory in his holy name;
let the hearts of those who seek the LORD rejoice.
Look to the LORD and his strength;
seek his face always.

✿ **PSALM 105:3-4**

The name of the LORD is a strong tower;
the righteous run to it and are safe.

✿ **PROVERBS 18:10**

Devotional Thought on

Strength

WARRIOR WOMAN

Deborah stood out as a strong, brave, smart and trustworthy woman among the people of her day. She believed God and obeyed his leading.

As a judge, Deborah heard the disputes of the Israelites and she solved their problems. She also helped them know God's will.

Deborah was doing something unusual for women in her day. She judged while most women were at home weaving. She prophesied when other women were cooking meals. And she went into battle while other women stayed home with the children.

The important thing, though, is not what Deborah did but whom she followed. Deborah willingly did whatever God asked of her. She would have been just as willing stay at home with the kids. But God called her into battle. Deborah didn't argue or make excuses. She simply obeyed, and God gave her incredible strength. God desires the same obedience from us, and when we obey, he will provide us the strength to do what he asks of us!

God's Words of Life on

Trust

When I am afraid,
I will trust in you.
In God, whose word I praise,
in God I trust; I will not be afraid.
What can mortal man do to me?

✿ PSALM 56:3-4

Trust in the LORD with all you heart
and lean not on your own understanding;
in all your ways acknowledge him,
and he will make your paths straight.

✿ PROVERBS 3:5-6

Let him who walks in the dark,
who has no light,
trust in the name of the LORD
and rely on his God.

✿ ISAIAH 50:10

Those who know your name will trust in you,
for you, LORD, have never forsaken those who
seek you.

✿ PSALM 9:10

God's Words of Life on

Trust

The LORD is good,
a refuge in times of trouble.
He cares for those who trust in him.

✿ **NAHUM 1:7**

Let the morning bring me word of your unfailing love,
for I have put my trust in you.
Show me the way I should go,
for to you I lift up my soul.

✿ **PSALM 143:8**

Commit your way to the LORD;
trust in him and he will do this:
He will make your righteousness shine like the dawn,
the justice of your cause like the noonday sun.

✿ **PSALM 37:5-6**

Those who trust in the LORD are like Mount Zion,
which cannot be shaken but endures forever.

✿ **PSALM 125:1**

God's Words of Life on

Trust

*You will keep in perfect peace, LORD,
    him whose mind is steadfast,
    because he trusts in you.*

❀ ISAIAH 26:3

*I am still confident of this:
    I will see the goodness of the LORD
    in the land of the living.
Wait for the LORD;
    be strong and take heart
    and wait for the LORD.*

❀ PSALM 27:13-14

*Trust in the LORD forever,
    for the LORD, the LORD, is the Rock eternal.*

❀ ISAIAH 26:4

God's Words of Life on

Trust

Surely this is our God;
we trusted in him, and he saved us.
This is the LORD, we trusted in him;
let us rejoice and be glad in his salvation.

✿ ISAIAH 25:9

So this is what the Sovereign LORD says:
"See, I lay a stone in Zion,
a tested stone,
a precious cornerstone for a sure foundation;
the one who trusts will never be dismayed."

✿ ISAIAH 28:16

Jesus said, "Do not let your hearts be troubled. Trust
in God; trust also in me."

✿ JOHN 14:1

In repentance and rest is your salvation,
in quietness and trust is your strength.

✿ ISAIAH 30:15

God's Words of Life on

Trust

Blessed is the man who trusts in the LORD,
whose confidence is in him.
He will be like a tree planted by the water
that sends out its roots by the stream.
It does not fear when heat comes;
its leaves are always green.
It has no worries in a year of drought
and never fails to bear fruit.

✿ JEREMIAH 17:7-8

Anyone who trusts in Jesus will never be put to shame.

✿ ROMANS 10:11

May the God of hope fill you with all joy and peace as you trust in him, so that you may overflow with hope by the power of the Holy Spirit.

✿ ROMANS 15:13

Devotional Thought on

Trust

TRUSTING GOD IN HARD TIMES

People around the prophet Habakkuk are doing wrong things, and Habakkuk wonders why God is letting it happen. God tells Habakkuk that he won't let it go on forever. He is going to punish the people for the wrong things they have done. So Habakkuk decides to trust God's wisdom and to rejoice, no matter how bad things get.

All through life, many situations, things and people will test your faith in God. Habakkuk decides that whatever happens, he will keep trusting God. If you believe in Jesus, you have the Holy Spirit to help you keep trusting God, too, no matter what.

Write this verse on a little card: "The LORD is good, a refuge in times of trouble. He cares for those who trust in him" (Nahum 1:7). Try to memorize this verse. The next time you are having a hard time or are being tested, let this verse remind you to trust God.

God's Words of Life on

Wisdom

The fear of the LORD is the beginning of wisdom,
and knowledge of the Holy One is understanding.

✿ PROVERBS 9:10

The wisdom that comes from heaven is first of all
pure; then peace-loving, considerate, submissive, full
of mercy and good fruit, impartial and sincere.

✿ JAMES 3:17

He who walks with the wise grows wise.

✿ PROVERBS 13:20

Know also that wisdom is sweet to your soul;
if you find it, there is a future hope for you,
and your hope will not be cut off.

✿ PROVERBS 24:14

If any of you lacks wisdom, he should ask God, who
gives generously to all without finding fault, and it
will be given to him.

✿ JAMES 1:5

God's Words of Life on

Wisdom

Praise be to the name of God for ever and ever;
*   wisdom and power are his.*
He changes times and seasons;
*   he sets up kings and deposes them.*
He gives wisdom to the wise
*   and knowledge to the discerning.*

❀ **DANIEL 2:20-21**

I keep asking that the God of our Lord Jesus Christ,
the glorious Father, may give you the Spirit of wisdom
and revelation, so that you may know him better.

❀ **EPHESIANS 1:17**

Get wisdom, get understanding;
*   do not forget my words or swerve from them.*
Do not forsake wisdom, and she will protect you;
*   love her, and she will watch over you.*
Wisdom is supreme, therefore get wisdom.
*   Though it cost all you have, get understanding.*

❀ **PROVERBS 4:5-7**

God's Words of Life on

Wisdom

Teach us to number our days aright, O LORD,
that we may gain a heart of wisdom.

❁ PSALM 90:12

Surely you desire truth in the inner parts, LORD;
you teach me wisdom in the inmost place.

❁ PSALM 51:6

Wisdom, like an inheritance, is a good thing
and benefits those who see the sun.
Wisdom is a shelter
as money is a shelter,
but the advantage of knowledge is this:
that wisdom preserves the life of its possessor.

❁ ECCLESIASTES 7:11-12

He who gets wisdom loves his own soul;
he who cherishes understanding prospers.

❁ PROVERBS 19:8

God's Words of Life on

Wisdom

A wife of noble character who can find?
She ... works with eager hands. ...
She gets up while it is still dark;
*   she provides food for her family. ...*
She sets about her work vigorously;
*   her arms are strong for her tasks. ...*
She opens her arms to the poor
*   and extends her hands to the needy.*
When it snows, she has no fear for her household;
*   for all of them are clothed in scarlet. ...*
She is clothed with strength and dignity;
*   she can laugh at the days to come.*
She speaks with wisdom,
*   and faithful instruction is on her tongue. ...*
Her children arise and call her blessed;
*   her husband also, and he praises her:*
"Many women do noble things,
*   but you surpass them all."*
Charm is deceptive, and beauty is fleeting;
*   but a woman who fears the LORD is to be*
praised.

✿ PROVERBS 31:10, 13, 15, 17, 20-21,
   25-26, 28-30

God's Words of Life on

Wisdom

If you call out for insight
and cry aloud for understanding,
and if you look for it as for silver
and search for it as for hidden treasure,
then you will understand the fear of the LORD
and find the knowledge of God.

✿ **PROVERBS 2:3-5**

Those who are wise will shine like the brightness of
the heavens, and those who lead many to righteous-
ness, like the stars for ever and ever.

✿ **DANIEL 12:3**

The fear of the LORD is the beginning of wisdom;
all who follow his precepts
have good understanding.
To him belongs eternal praise.

✿ **PSALM 111:10**

Devotional Thought on

Wisdom

BUILDING A HOUSE

Making a good life is a little like building a house. What kinds of things would you have to do if you were planning to build a dollhouse for your favorite doll or teddy bear? You'd need a good plan to follow. And maybe you'd even want to look at models to get ideas for how you want your house to look. How many rooms would it have? Would there be a really big living room or kitchen? Then, you start shopping for furniture and other things to make it feel like home.

God has given Christians a plan for building their lives. He has even given them a model. The plan is the commands he gives us in the Bible. And Jesus is the model. Christians want to follow this example of love, kindness, forgiving others, and unselfishness.

To build a good life you can ask for God's help. God will help you by giving you his wisdom and his power to help you do it! But you don't become wise by sitting in front of the TV. God enjoys giving you wisdom. If you go to him for it, you will get it.

God's Words of Life on

Work

May the favor of the LORD our God rest upon us;
establish the work of our hands for us—
yes, establish the work of our hands.

✿ **PSALM 90:17**

Whatever you do, work at it with all your heart, as
working for the Lord, not for men, since you know
that you will receive an inheritance from the Lord as
a reward. It is the Lord Christ you are serving.

✿ **COLOSSIANS 3:23-24**

The man who plants and the man who waters have
one purpose, and each will be rewarded according to
his own labor. For we are God's fellow workers; you
are God's field, God's building.

✿ **1 CORINTHIANS 3:8-9**

God is not unjust; he will not forget your work and
the love you have shown him as you have helped his
people and continue to help them.

✿ **HEBREWS 6:10**

God's Words of Life on

Work

We are God's workmanship, created in Christ Jesus to do good works, which God prepared in advance for us to do.

✿ EPHESIANS 2:10

Whatever you do, whether in word or deed, do it all in the name of the Lord Jesus, giving thanks to God the Father through him.

✿ COLOSSIANS 3:17

Six days you shall labor and do all your work, but the seventh day is a Sabbath to the LORD your God. On it you shall not do any work.

✿ DEUTERONOMY 5:13-14

Serve wholeheartedly, as if you were serving the Lord, not men, because you know that the Lord will reward everyone for whatever good he does.

✿ EPHESIANS 6:7-8

God's Words of Life on

Work

My heart took delight in all my work,
*   and this was the reward for all my labor.*

✿ ECCLESIASTES 2:10

Blessed are all who fear the LORD,
*   who walk in his ways.*
You will eat the fruit of your labor;
*   blessings and prosperity will be yours.*

✿ PSALM 128:1-2

By hard work we must help the weak, remembering
the words the Lord Jesus himself said: "It is more
blessed to give than to receive."

✿ ACTS 20:35

The plans of the diligent lead to profit.

✿ PROVERBS 21:5

The LORD your God has blessed you in all the work
of your hands.

✿ DEUTERONOMY 2:7

Devotional Thought on

Work

WHAT WOULD YOU LIKE TO DO?

Reading through the last chapter of Proverbs hightlights the many different kinds of work women can do. Using different gifts, talents and areas of
wisdom fulfill God's plan. This chapter gives a few ideas of where a young woman like you can start.

Read through all the things done by the wife in Proverbs 31. Then pick out some that sound like things you might like to do. It's never too early to start exploring your talents and learning about the kinds of work that you might like you to do. Check out this list of things that the woman in Proverbs 31 did:

- ✿ She picks out fabrics and makes things from it. (v. 13)
- ✿ She goes out and gets cool, special food from far-away places to make fun meals. (v. 14)
- ✿ She teaches younger girls the best way to do things around the house. (v. 15)
- ✿ She helps those who don't have much. (v. 20)
- ✿ She sells the things she makes at the market. (v. 24)
- ✿ She teaches her children to be wise and kind. (v. 26)
- ✿ Her kids and husband think she's the best, and so does God! (v. 28-31)

God's Words of Life on

Worry

Jesus said, "Do not worry about your life, what you will eat or drink; or about your body, what you will wear. Is not life more important than food, and the body more important than clothes? Look at the birds of the air; they do not sow or reap or store away in barns, and yet your heavenly Father feeds them. Are you not much more valuable than they?"

✿ MATTHEW 6:25-26

Why are you downcast, O my soul?
    Why so disturbed within me?
Put your hope in God,
    for I will yet praise him,
    my Savior and my God.

✿ PSALM 42:11

Cast your cares on the LORD
    and he will sustain you;
    he will never let the righteous fall.

✿ PSALM 55:22

God's Words of Life on

Worry

*Trust in the L*ORD *and do good;*
dwell in the land and enjoy safe pasture.
*Delight yourself in the L*ORD
and he will give you the desires of your heart.

✿ PSALM 37:3-4

Do not be anxious about anything, but in every-
thing, by prayer and petition, with thanksgiving,
present your requests to God. And the peace of God,
which transcends all understanding, will guard your
hearts and your minds in Christ Jesus.

✿ PHILIPPIANS 4:6-7

Cast all your anxiety on God because he cares
for you.

✿ 1 PETER 5:7

*If the L*ORD *delights in a man's way,*
he makes his steps firm;
though he stumble, he will not fall,
*for the L*ORD *upholds him with his hand.*

✿ PSALM 37:23-24

God's Words of Life on

Worry

When I said, "My foot is slipping,"
your love, O LORD, supported me.
When anxiety was great within me,
your consolation brought joy to my soul.

✿ **PSALM 94:18-19**

God is just: He will pay back trouble to those who
trouble you and give relief to you who are troubled,
and to us as well. This will happen when the Lord
Jesus is revealed from heaven in blazing fire with his
powerful angels.

✿ **2 THESSALONIANS 1:6-7**

The LORD is faithful to all his promises
and loving toward all he has made.
The LORD upholds all those who fall
and lifts up all who are bowed down.

✿ **PSALM 145:13-14**

Surely God is my help;
the LORD is the one who sustains me.

✿ **PSALM 54:4**

God's Words of Life on

Worry

Let all who take refuge in you be glad;
*   let them ever sing for joy.*
Spread your protection over them,
*   that those who love your name may rejoice in you.*
For surely, O LORD, you bless the righteous;
*   you surround them with your favor as*
*   with a shield.*

✿ PSALM 5:11-12

Praise be to the LORD, to God our Savior,
*   who daily bears our burdens.*

✿ PSALM 68:19

"When you pass through the waters,
*   I will be with you;*
and when you pass through the rivers,
*   they will not sweep over you.*
When you walk through the fire,
*   you will not be burned;*
*   the flames will not set you ablaze," says the LORD.*

✿ ISAIAH 43:2

God's Words of Life on

Worry

In my alarm I said,
"I am cut off from your sight!"
Yet you heard my cry for mercy
when I called to you for help.
Love the LORD, all his saints!
The LORD preserves the faithful.

✿ PSALM 31:22-23

Jesus said, "Why do you worry about clothes? See how the lilies of the field grow. They do not labor or spin. Yet I tell you that not even Solomon in all his splendor was dressed like one of these. If that is how God clothes the grass of the field, which is here today and tomorrow is thrown into the fire, will he not much more clothe you? ... So do not worry, saying, 'What shall we eat?' or 'What shall we drink?' or 'What shall we wear?' For ... your heavenly Father knows that you need them. But seek first his kingdom and his righteousness, and all these things will be given to you as well. Therefore do not worry about tomorrow, for tomorrow will worry about itself. Each day has enough trouble of its own."

✿ MATTHEW 6:28-34

Devotional Thought on

Worry

DON'T WORRY ... REST!

God rested on the seventh day after he created the world. He set aside this day for his people to rest, too. The writer of Hebrews says that God has created a rest that every believer can enter, no matter what problems they face.

When we encounter unexpected pain or trouble, we tend to get stressed and upset. But when we step back and give God control to deal with our situation, he gives us the peace to endure it. Philippians 4:6-8 says that we don't have to worry about anything. We should bring our worries to God and in exchange he will give us peace that is so wonderful, no one can understand it. So, don't worry ... rest in God!

God's Words of Life on

Worship

Jesus said, "A time is coming and has now come when the true worshipers will worship the Father in spirit and truth, for they are the kind of worshipers the Father seeks."

✿ JOHN 4:23

Worship the LORD with gladness;
*   come before him with joyful songs. ...*
Enter his gates with thanksgiving
*   and his courts with praise;*
*   give thanks to him and praise his name.*
For the LORD is good and his love endures forever;
*   his faithfulness continues through all generations.*

✿ PSALM 100:2, 4-5

Come, let us bow down in worship,
*   let us kneel before the LORD our Maker;*
for he is our God
*   and we are the people of his pasture,*
*   the flock under his care.*

✿ PSALM 95:6-7

God's Words of Life on

Worship

Since we are receiving a kingdom that cannot be shaken, let us be thankful, and so worship God acceptably with reverence and awe.

✿ **HEBREWS 12:28**

I will praise you, O LORD my God, with all my heart;
I will glorify your name forever.
For great is your love toward me.

✿ **PSALM 86:12-13**

Let the heavens rejoice, let the earth be glad;
let them say among the nations, "The LORD reigns!"
Let the sea resound, and all that is in it;
let the fields be jubilant, and everything in them!
Then the trees of the forest will sing,
they will sing for joy before the LORD,
for he comes to judge the earth.
Give thanks to the LORD, for he is good;
his love endures forever.

✿ **1 CHRONICLES 16:31-34**

God's Words of Life on

Worship

Stand up and praise the LORD your God, who is from everlasting to everlasting. Blessed be your glorious name, and may it be exalted above all blessing and praise. You alone are the LORD. You made the heavens, even the highest heavens, and all their starry host, the earth and all that is on it, the seas and all that is in them. You give life to everything, and the multitudes of heaven worship you.

✿ NEHEMIAH 9:5-6

In the day of my trouble I will call to you,
    for you will answer me.
Among the gods there is none like you, O LORD;
    no deeds can compare with yours.
All the nations you have made
     will come and worship before you, O LORD;
    they will bring glory to your name.
For you are great and do marvelous deeds;
    you alone are God.

✿ PSALM 86:7-10

God's Words of Life on

Worship

I have seen you in the sanctuary
and beheld your power and your glory.
Because your love is better than life,
my lips will glorify you.

✿ **PSALM 63:2-4**

Ascribe to the LORD, O families of nations,
Ascribe to the LORD glory and strength,
Ascribe to the LORD the glory due his name.
Bring an offering and come before him;
Worship the LORD in the splendor of his holiness.

✿ **1 CHRONICLES 16:28-29**

All the angels were standing around the throne and
around the elders and the four living creatures. They
fell down on their faces before the throne and worshiped God, saying: "Amen! Praise and glory and
wisdom and thanks and honor and power and
strength be to our God for ever and ever. Amen!"

✿ **REVELATION 7:11-12**

God's Words of Life on

Worship

Jesus said, "A time is coming and has now come when the true worshipers will worship the Father in spirit and truth, for they are the kind of worshipers the Father seeks. God is spirit, and his worshipers must worship in spirit and in truth."

✿ **JOHN 4:23-24**

...Those who had been victorious...held harps given them by God and sang the song of Moses the servant of God and the song of the Lamb: "Great and marvelous are your deeds, Lord God Almighty. Just and true are your ways, King of the ages. Who will not fear you, O Lord, and bring glory to your name? For you alone are holy. All nations will come and worship before you, for your righteous acts have been revealed."

✿ **REVELATION 15:2-4**

Praise the LORD. How good it is to sing praises to our God, how pleasant and fitting to praise him!

✿ **PSALM 147:1**

206

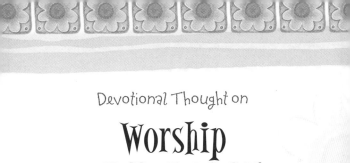

Devotional Thought on

Worship

OVER-THE-TOP WORSHIP

In Luke 7:36-50 we read about a woman who worships in a way that others say is over the top. A woman crashes a dinner party where Jesus is eating with an important church official. She washes Jesus' feet with her own tears and wipes them clean with her hair. Then she pours expensive perfume on them. The rest of the people in the room are offended by this woman, but Jesus sees that she loves him more than anyone else in that room and she is willing to show it, no matter what others think of her.

Sometimes the way you worship may cause others to wrinkle up their noses and walk away. But don't let what other people might think or say keep you from expressing the joy and love you feel in your heart. Praising God makes your heavenly Father happy.

Get excited about God's gift of eternal life. Whatever your style, wherever you are, always be praising him!

Other Titles to Enjoy from Inspirio:

*God's Words of Life for Students from the
New International Version*

*God's Words of Life for Teens from the
New International Version*

*You, God, & Real Life
A Survivor's Guide*

Promises for Students from the New International Version

*For the Graduate
God's Guidance for the Road Ahead
Bright Hope for Your Future*